ARIS AND PHILLIPS HISPANIC CLASSICS

JOSÉ DÍAZ-FERNÁNDEZ

THE BLOCKHOUSE

(El blocao)

Edited by

Adolfo Campoy-Cubillo

Translated by

Paul Southern

Aris & Phillips is an imprint of Oxbow Books

Published in the United Kingdom in 2016 by
OXBOW BOOKS
10 Hythe Bridge Street, Oxford OX1 2EW

and in the United States by
OXBOW BOOKS
1950 Lawrence Road, Havertown, PA 19083

Hardback Edition: ISBN 978-1-91057-228-3
Paperback Edition: ISBN 978-1-91057-214-6
Digital Edition: ISBN 978-1-91057-215-3

A CIP record for this book is available from the British Library

For a complete list of Aris & Phillips titles, please contact:

UNITED KINGDOM	UNITED STATES OF AMERICA
Oxbow Books	Oxbow Books
Telephone (01865) 241249	Telephone (800) 791-9354
Fax (01865) 794449	Fax (610) 853-9146
Email: oxbow@oxbowbooks.com	Email: queries@casemateacademic.com
www.oxbowbooks.com	www.casemateacademic.com/oxbow

Oxbow Books is part of the Casemate group

Printed and bound in Great Britain by
Marston Book Services Ltd, Oxfordshire

Front cover: Travel views of Morocco by Arnold Genthe, 1869–1942. Library of Congress,
Prints & Photographs Division, Arnold Genthe Collection: Negatives and Transparencies,
[LC-G396-0005]

CONTENTS

INTRODUCTION

The publication of José Díaz-Fernández's *El blocao. Novela de la guerra marroquí* in 1928 was received enthusiastically both by the critics and the public at large. Díaz-Fernández's novel went through three editions in less than two years. This was certainly not a minor feat if one considers that the editors of Historia Nueva, the publishing house where *El blocao* appeared, had always believed that their company would be bankrupt within one or two years (Santonja 1986, 205). To everyone's surprise, including the author's, *El blocao* struck a chord with Spaniards from all walks of life. The success of *El blocao* must be understood in the context of the highly idiosyncratic position that Spain found itself in at the turn of the twentieth century. Spain had been struggling to take control of the northern Morocco territories that constituted the Spanish Protectorate for over a decade; its inability to succeed was symptomatic of the profound identity crisis that the country had undergone after the loss of its colonies in the nineteenth century, and the deep-seated corruption that had rendered the Spanish military inefficient. Díaz-Fernández's novel managed to circumvent censorship regulations and provide a much needed critique of Spain's colonial enterprise in northern Africa. His novel was a response to a specific moment in Spanish history, but this response was informed by his deep understanding of European political realities during the interwar period. Díaz-Fernández was a keen observer of international politics and was equally interested in the cultural production of the European avant-gardes that preceded him. In *El blocao*, Díaz-Fernández managed to combine elements that seemed irreconcilable: a political critique of Spain's involvement in Africa presented in the experimental language of the avant-garde but still able to appeal to the public at large.

By 1898, Spain had lost the last colony of its once huge empire. The loss of Cuba and the rest of the American and Asian Spanish colonies was not only an economic catastrophe, but also a tremendous blow to the national pride of the Spanish people that struggled to articulate a coherent, post-imperial identity. Spanish intellectuals tried to diagnose the causes of the country's decadence in an effort to regenerate its vigor in the belief that Spain could regain its position in the new world order. Africa, and more specifically Morocco, seemed to provide the opportunity Spain needed for imperial regeneration. Its geographical proximity, allied to the historical connection between the Spanish and Moroccan peoples were, in the mind

of the Spanish *Africanista* colonialist leaders, clear signs that Spain was destined to play a more active role in the colonization of north Africa.

By the time the Spanish Empire began to disintegrate during the eighteenth century, the main European nations had already developed empires of their own. Great Britain led the way, followed by France, Germany and Belgium. European imperialist expansion occupied territories in North and Central America, and Asia, but avoided venturing into Africa. By 1880, however, the colonization of Africa became the main objective of most European powers. In a relatively short period of time (1881–1914), Europe partitioned and occupied most of the African continent. The reasons for this delayed, but suddenly acute interest in Africa are complex and manifold, and there is no clear consensus among historians about what was the main cause that triggered what became known as the Scramble for Africa. Explanations of the causes for this sudden interest in Africa can be divided into three main categories: economic, psychological, and diplomatic (Boahen 1990, 10–5). The economic explanation represented by the work of Hobson (1902), Hilferding (1910), Luxemburg (1913, 1915), Bukharin (1915, 1924), and Lenin (1916) argues that with the advent of the industrial revolution, Europe needed to open new markets that could absorb its excess of production. Historians that subscribe to this hypothesis explain that colonialism was a natural outcome of capitalism. Psychological interpretations of colonialism were pioneered by Joseph Schumpeter who explained that Europeans perceived themselves as racially and culturally superior to the peoples they colonized, and that it was this belief in European superiority that led them to occupy other continents, including Africa. Finally, the diplomatic theory, represented among others by Carlton Hayes, argues that colonial expansion was a question of national prestige, and that colonial possessions became a very valuable bargaining chip in turn-of-the-century Europe. There is ample evidence for all three theories, and the colonization of Africa can certainly be explained as a combination of all three. Nationalist discourses were often used to promote specific economic interests. Similarly, nationalist pride led most colonialists to believe that European civilization was the only possible outcome of progress, which meant that any other non-Western civilization was out of pace with history and hence in need of intervention.

The partition of Africa among the different European powers aimed to avoid conflicts that could lead to a war among the colonizing nations. As part of this more or less orderly partition of the African territories, Britain and France signed in 1904 the Entente Cordiale, an accord by which each

country agreed to respect the areas of influence of each other's empire. Among the many issues settled, it was agreed that Britain would continue the colonization of Egypt while France would occupy Morocco. Conflicts, however, did arise and Morocco became one of the main scenarios where those conflicts were to be resolved. One of the results of the Entente Cordiale was that in reconciling their colonial interests, France and Britain had become allies against German expansion in Africa. Germany, as could be expected, was not willing to accept this disadvantageous position. In 1905, Kaiser Wilhelm II visited Tangier and made a series of public statements regarding his support for the independence of Morocco, which was interpreted as an explicit expression of interest in the colonization of Morocco on the part of Germany. France was outraged by what it considered a threat to its own interests in Morocco, and Britain was ready to take sides with the French to protect its interests in north Africa. The Algeciras Conference was convened to negotiate the colonization of the territory. There was, however, very little room for negotiations since only one of two options could prevail. In the end, France, with the support of Britain, succeeded in claiming Morocco thereby securing its control of north Africa. Germany was forced to abandon all plans to occupy Morocco; its relations with France and Britain were seriously strained. Spain, on the other hand, was allowed to pursue its interests in Morocco. The decision of the European powers to support the project of a Spanish Protectorate was perceived by the Spanish government as a vindication of its historical rights. France and Britain, however, were not as concerned with Spain's historical rights over Morocco as with securing the strategic status quo. In this sense, Spain was clearly the best option; Spanish control of northern Morocco was to act as a buffer against British influence in the area without compromising France's control of the region. Spain represented a weak colonial power that should not, in the calculation of the British and French, interfere with their own colonial agenda.

The agreements reached at the Algeciras Conference, however, did not entirely appease Germany's desire to intervene in Morocco. In 1911, Kinderlen complained about the political chaos in French-controlled Morocco which was, in his opinion, endangering German economic interests in the area. Spaniards were also complaining about the limited access to the country's resources that the partition of Morocco had granted them, and the stability of the Protectorate seemed to be in question. The Germans sent the gunboat *Panther* to Agadir and demanded compensation from France. Germany was hoping that France's military weakness and Britain's political

instability resulting from the constitutional crisis caused by the rejection of the 1909 budget by the House of Lords would play in its favor and allow it to either break the alliance between Britain and France, take control of part of Morocco, or both. The Second Moroccan Crisis, as the conflict came to be known, confirmed Britain's support of France and Germany's isolation. France agreed to grant Germany control over two strips of land in French Congo, but Germany had to agree to a French protectorate over Morocco (Burke 1976, 171–3). Germany's national pride had been hurt once more, and it decided to arm itself in preparation for what it considered an inevitable war. World War I would eventually begin as a result of Germany's support of Austro-Hungary after the assassination of Archduke Franz Ferdinand, but the alignment of forces had already been articulated during the two Moroccan Crises.

Germany's struggles to participate in the Scramble for Africa have traditionally been described as a family feud between Kaiser Wilhelm II and the other European royal families to which he was related since he was the grandson of Queen Victoria (Clay 2006). The interests of the different European monarchies were certainly interwoven, and marriages and kinship had often been used as a way to promote political agendas. The family-feud interpretation, however, tends to depend heavily on the importance of personal character. These accounts present Wilhelm as a spoiled, young man obsessed with military parades and imperial glory. Wilhelm's own account of the events in his memoirs suggests that the visit to Morocco was the idea of his chancellor which he initially objected to, but finally "gave in, with a heavy heart, for I feared that this visit, in view of the situation at Paris, might be construed as a provocation and cause an inclination in London to support France in case of war" (Wilhelm II 1922, 108). Of course, Wilhelm II's account tries to avoid blame for the actions that eventually led to World War I, Germany's defeat, and the demise of the German monarchy and the Austro-Hungarian Empire. The family-feud interpretation of the two Moroccan crises, however, is also an attempt to present European (French, British and even Spanish and Portuguese) colonialism as moderate and rational as opposed to German irrational and temperamental colonialism.

The colonization of Africa presented two different models: on the one hand Britain and France followed a liberal model; on the other hand Germany developed its own Weltpolitik which was closer to the mercantilist model. This often meant that British and French governments worked in close collaboration with private companies to develop commercial networks

in their colonies while Germany pursued a much more centralized type of colonization (Conrad 2012, 64). It also meant that liberal thinkers had to reconcile the concepts of human dignity around which liberalism had been articulated with the inhuman conditions that colonization created for those peoples it colonized. The psychological factor alluded to before is probably the best explanation of how this contradiction was resolved. European liberals wanted dignity for all peoples, but perceived non-Europeans as backward and in need of colonization to attain what they deemed to be a dignified status (Pitts 2005, 5).

Spain, particularly after 1914, was divided in two large groups: those that considered themselves Germanophiles and those that sided with the Allies. Although the line that separated one group from the other was at times unclear, Germanophiles were for the most part traditionalists that saw in Germany a protection against liberalism. The Spanish military, the Carlistas, and Mauristas were traditionalists and consequently Germanophiles, but some Spanish liberals like philosopher Ortega y Gasset were fascinated by German culture as well. Despite the pervasive presence of traditionalism in Spanish society and politics, liberalism had had a long if conflictive history in Spain. The proclamation of the 1812 Spanish Constitution, one of the earliest and most liberal constitutions in Europe, a model that inspired liberals in Italy, Germany, Russia, and Latin America, was certainly a benchmark in the evolution of liberalism. Liberal ideas, however, arrived too early to Spain. Despite the existence of a liberal intellectual elite, and even members of the aristocracy that were willing to go along with liberal reform, Spain's traditionalists greatly outnumbered the liberals. The result, as Stanley Payne has argued, is what has come to be known as the 'Spanish contradiction': "the persistent efforts of small, liberal or radical elites to introduce 'advanced' systems which lacked an adequate social, cultural, or economic base" (Payne 1967, 145). This contradiction applied not only to the political and economic organization of the Iberian Peninsula, but to the attempts of the Spanish government to pursue its colonial agenda. The Spanish colonial project in Morocco became an amalgam of private enterprise interests (especially the iron ore mines), demands for colonial expansion from the military, and an ambivalent role on the part of the Spanish government. If liberal colonization was normally characterized by the coordinated efforts of the business sector, the military, and the government, in the case of the Spanish Protectorate of Morocco, each of these entities seemed to have been acting independently of the other two. In the minds of the Spanish people,

including large sections of the military, Morocco became synonymous not with a national project of regeneration through colonization, as it had initially been intended, but with the defense of the economic interest of a small group within the Spanish upper bourgeoisie. The large number of casualties produced by the efforts to pacify the Spanish Protectorate made the Moroccan campaigns even more unpopular; a problem aggravated by the fact that most of the soldiers who died in the colonial wars belonged to the working class since the sons of the upper classes could afford to pay a 'quota' to secure a safe posting. In 1921, the Disaster of Annual during which Spanish troops were surrounded by Riffian leader, Abd el-Krim, resulted in the loss of over 13,000 men. The Picasso Report compiled to investigate how the massacre had been allowed to happen, revealed pervasive problems of corruption in an underequipped army. The colonial officers also became estranged from the central government that was often unwilling to pursue the aggressive expansion that the *Africanista* career soldiers would have preferred to undertake. The radicalization of the colonial officers was basically motivated by their unwillingness to abandon the opportunity for rapid promotion that the Spanish Protectorate represented. Any effort to slow down or halt the colonization of Spanish Morocco was resented by them. The dispute between the colonial officers and the Spanish government also came to have an ideological component. Most colonial officers were staunchly traditionalist, and viewed the liberal bourgeoisie and the leftist leaders of the Spanish Second Republic with disdain. It was precisely the colonial officers who organized the coup d'état that eventually led to the Spanish Civil War.

The Spanish Protectorate of Morocco, consequently, lacked a firm colonial agenda. Neither liberals nor entirely mercantilists, the Spanish colonial authorities seemed to have left part of the planning to improvisation. This somewhat chaotic approach to colonization was in part motivated by the lack of economic resources that the Spanish governments of the time had to deal with. As Moroccan historian Mimoun Aziza has argued, the Spanish Protectorate implemented a 'poor man's colonization'. Rather than bringing a modern lifestyle to the colonized, Spaniards led very similar lives to those led by Moroccans. "[T]here were no segregated neighborhoods as happened in the French zone," and, with the exception of the top brass and colonial administration, Spaniards and Moroccans shared the same limited resources (Aziza 2003, 257). This sense of comradeship between the colonizers and the colonized was certainly enhanced by conscious decisions on the part of the

Spanish colonial authorities. For instance, Spaniards, unlike the French who promoted the teaching of the French language among Moroccans, allowed Arabic to be taught in their schools. The psychological element that informed the Spanish colonization of Morocco was also different from that of other European powers. Spain did not argue its fitness for colonizing Morocco on the grounds of cultural superiority, but rather on the grounds of its cultural affinity with the Arab peoples who, lest we forget, had ruled the Iberian Peninsula for almost eight centuries. Historian Gustau Nerín has coined the term Hispanotropicalism to describe this type of colonization through cultural fraternity: the idea that the colonized is attached to the colonizer by an emotional bond of cultural brotherhood (Nerín 1998, 11). The notion of Hispano-tropicalism, of course, describes the way that Spaniards understood their own colonization, and not the way that colonization was perceived by the Moroccan people.

Morocco, as could be expected, became a popular topic in Spanish literature at the turn of the century. *Modernismo*, the literary movement that was in vogue in the Spanish-speaking world at that time, advocated a highly estheticizing exoticism for which Morocco was perfectly fitted. Rubén Darío said about his visit to Tangier in *Tierras solares*: "I feel, for the first time as if I were in the setting for one of my favorite books [*One Thousand and One Nights*]" (Darío 1904, 150). Among the Spanish *modernistas*, Isaac Muñoz made the Maghreb,[1] the central theme of his entire literary career. The novels and poems of Isaac Muñoz presented the Maghreb as a mysterious land where Spaniards could reconnect with the primal vigor that their nation had lost in 1898. His exotic descriptions of Moroccan life alternated with highly detailed analyses of the best approach for a colonization of Morocco. Like many of his contemporaries, Muñoz was able to entertain both the lofty rhetoric of Orientalism and the objective analysis of the economic advantages that an expansion of Spain in Morocco would engender. On the opposite side of the political spectrum, Ramón María del Valle-Inclán published *La pipa de kif* (1919), a collection of poems that exalted the liberating and revolutionary power of the drug popularized in Spain by Spanish travelers to Morocco. If the savage brutality of the Moroccan traditions described by Muñoz was supposed to allow Spaniards to reconnect with the primal will to power that Nietzsche had described in *Beyond Good and Evil* in 1886, the sensual view of the world induced by smoking kif was, according to Valle-

---

[1] The Maghreb is the name used to designate the region that includes Mauritania, Algeria, Morocco, Western Sahara, Libya, and Tunisia.

Inclán, capable of subverting traditionalist conventions and allowing for a more egalitarian culture (Fuentes 1987, 173–5).

The traumatic death of thousands of young Spanish men at the Disaster of Annual contributed to the radicalization the positions of those for and against the colonization of Morocco. Spaniards were not only shocked by the loss of life, but humiliated by the fact that a non-professional army of Berber rebels had been able to defeat them. In 1923, Ernesto Giménez-Caballero published *Notas marruecas de un soldado*, a literary account of his own experiences in Morocco. The book was an ambivalent denunciation of the problems of corruption and lack of political support that the Spanish colonial troops endured in the Protectorate. Giménez-Caballero was not complaining about Spain's involvement in north Africa. On the contrary, he considered that Spain should be much more active in establishing its presence in the Maghreb, but that Spanish politicians were not providing the military with enough support. His denunciation of irregularities in the administration of the Protectorate, however, came at an extremely sensitive time. The Picasso Report stopped short of accusing King Alfonso XIII of participating in the overall corruption that had mired the Spanish military, and Giménez-Caballero was arrested and given an eighteen-year sentence. General Primo de Rivera's coup d'état saved him from serving his sentence. The coup was primarily motivated by the efforts of the military and the monarchy to put an end to the investigation, and Giménez-Caballero's book was understood as a vindication of the military's honor and a critique of liberal politicians. Giménez-Caballero combined the pseudo-journalistic reporting of his experiences with an estheticization of the situations that he described. Despite the uneven literary quality of the book, *Notas marruecas de un soldado* was certainly original in its ability to bring art to everyday reality. Giménez-Caballero's prose alternated between the direct style of journalistic reporting and the lyrical description of his experiences. Giménez-Caballero would eventually become the editor of *La Gaceta Literaria*, a literary journal that played a crucial role in the articulation and promotion of the Spanish avant-garde. In fact, he would become one of the few exponents of the avant-garde *Ultraista* movement as the co-editor of *La Gaceta Literaria*, and prestigious literary critic Guillermo De Torre, acknowledged (De Torre 1965, 571). One of the chief objectives of the avant-garde was precisely to estheticize ordinary reality in order to subvert it. Subversion, however, could go in many different directions; in the case of Giménez-Caballero and the avant-garde artists that became associated

with *La Gaceta Literaria*, the subversive power of avant-garde literature was aimed at promoting an authoritarian state.

Parallel to the elitist avant-garde movement, serial publications had been slowly appearing in Spain during the nineteenth century. By mid-century, the number of publications and the size of their print run increased significantly as technological improvements which had been tested throughout Europe, began to be adopted in Spain as well (Charnon-Deutsch 2008, 86). The new and growing mass cultural market that serial publications contributed to create, required a specific type of literary product that could attract the attention of the widest number of readers. The publication of serial novels and short stories that avoided literary sophistication in search of sensationalism soon became a cultural phenomenon. By the 1920s the Spanish Protectorate of Morocco had become a popular topic among these publications. Authors like Carlos Micó and Juan Ferragut combined action, heroic deeds, and romance against a backdrop of more or less remote, Moroccan scenarios. The serial novel on Morocco did not have a clear political agenda; writers were extremely sensitive to changes in public opinion as the war progressed. In general, we can see a transition from the inflammatory patriotism of the early stories to the more critical point of view of the later ones. In any case, criticism of the war is only expressed as a reaction to the elevated number of casualties on the Spanish side, and anti-colonialist views were rarely, if ever, articulated in the popular novel.

The Spanish avant-garde, like the European avant-gardes, saw itself as an elitist esthetic movement. It was, however, deeply informed by the mass cultural market defined by, among other things, the serial novels on the Moroccan war. Avant-garde artists were constantly seeking the attention of the mass market that they despised, often using polemics as a promotional tool. Giménez-Caballero's fearless denunciation of corruption in *Notas marruecas de un soldado*, which everybody knew could only result in a jail sentence for its author, is a clear example of this. During the 1920s, the subversive activity of the Spanish avant-gardes was complicated by the onset of the Primo de Rivera dictatorship that subjected all kinds of cultural production to strict censorship. Magazines were routinely censored or confiscated. Books of more than 200 pages, which made them expensive for the general public, were exempt from censorship, and avant-garde writers soon realized that their future was in book publishing rather than magazine editing. The *Post-Guerra* magazine, for example, with which José Díaz-Fernández collaborated, decided to create a publishing house, Ediciones

Oriente. Transforming the avant-garde magazines into publishing houses circumvented, at least temporarily, the problem of censorship, but, as the editors of Ediciones Oriente soon found out, the literary industry imposed its own restrictions. Book distributors refused to work with Ediciones Oriente due to its radical political views and their lack of trust in the commercial viability of their catalogue, and Ediciones Oriente had to resort to creating its own distributor agency (Santonja 1986, 171–8).

Despite all these difficulties, Ediciones Oriente soon realized that there was indeed a market for their catalogue and decided to create Historia Nueva, a second publishing house that would share resources with Ediciones Oriente, but concentrate on Spanish authors rather than foreign leftist authors as Ediciones Oriente did. Part of the commercial success of Ediciones Oriente and Historia Nueva was their ability to learn from the marketing techniques of the popular novel. Unlike other reputable publishers, they advertised the new titles in the press and began compiling a mailing list of all their clients offering them a subscription to receive each new book that was added to their catalogue. This form of direct sale allowed both publishing houses to capitalize their investment without needing to depend on outside investors (Santonja 1986, 201). The success of *El blocao* would have been unthinkable without the ability of its author and the publishers of Historia Nueva to circumvent the many challenges that literary production presented in 1920s Spain.

Díaz-Fernández had initially written *El blocao* as a short story that had been selected for the first prize in a literary competition organized by the Spanish daily *El Imparcial*. The new direction taken by the *Post-Guerra* group persuaded him to transform the initial short story into a book-long project. The book consists of seven short stories that describe life in Spanish Morocco from the perspective of Sergeant Arnedo, a one-time socialist activist who finds himself drafted to the African front after the 1921 Disaster of Annual. Each one of the seven short stories is a complete unit. They can be read in isolation. They also inform each other, as Díaz-Fernández explained in the prologue to the second edition of his novel, and to craft a narrative that is held together by the atmosphere that surrounds the events being described (Díaz-Fernández 1976, 27). *El blocao*, consequently, could easily appeal to the consumer of popular novels on Morocco, and to those who had been waiting for a critical account of the events.

This new type of literature that combined some of the innovations of the avant-garde with the critique of Spain's current events is what Díaz-Fernández

baptized with the name of *nuevo romanticismo* (new romanticism). The new movement defined itself in opposition to the frivolous, conservative, avant-garde writers like, among others, Giménez-Caballero who had been the center of attention of the literary world during the 1920s. The name, *nuevo romanticismo*, was a direct reference to Ortega y Gasset's complaint that all cultural production prior to the arrival of the dehumanized art of the avant-garde had just been populist romanticism. Ortega advocated an elitist art, an art produced by select minds to guide the way into a new era. Díaz-Fernández's response to Ortega was that what was needed was an art for the masses that helped articulate their needs and concerns, while preserving the rhetorical discoveries made by the avant-garde.

José Díaz-Fernández's literary career was brief. By 1930, he had already been elected parliamentarian for the Partido Radical Socialista. He remained more interested in political activism than in the endless competition for recognition that the literary world requires. After the success of *El blocao,* his manifesto *El nuevo romanticismo* was received with indifference, his second novel *La venus mecánica* had hardly any more success, and he lost all interest in pursuing his career as a novelist any further. He only took up the pen again to write, in collaboration with Joaquín Arderíus, a biography of Captain Fermín Galán,[2] and *Octubre rojo*, an account of the 1934 miners' strikes. In 1936, he was elected again as a parliamentarian for Izquierda Republicana, but the Francoist rebellion that led to the Spanish Civil War also truncated his political career. He died in exile in France in 1941, while many other Spanish writers and politicians who had also escaped to France, already under German control, were being sent to French concentration camps.

---

[2]   Captain Fermin Galán led the rebellion against the Primo de Rivera dictatorship in 1926, and the Jaca rebellion against the Spanish monarchy in 1930.

TRANSLATOR'S NOTE

As to be expected, a strong thread of military jargon runs throughout the novel, it gives credence to the voice of Díaz-Fernández's alter ego, the quota soldier Carlos Arnedo, without detriment to the general reader's comprehension of the stories. Military jargon, like any technical discourse, evolves over the years. An accurate translation required not only familiarity with English language military terminology, but most importantly, with the military terminology current at the time *El blocao* was written. A more neutral use of military vocabulary would have distorted the portrait of turn-of-the century Spanish colonial warfare presented by Díaz-Fernández. 'Cuota', a pivotal element in the stories, describes a military draft system without equivalent in the armies of the English speaking world. In order to retain the word and its vitally important concept it has been rendered as 'quota', with an explanatory footnote.

The author's use of imagery and metaphor presented challenges; challenges further complicated here by his often sophisticated sentence structure. Aware of the bilingual nature of the publication, the translator's task was to convey the sense of the author's words without distancing the reader from the original. Early examples are found on the first page of the first story 'The Blockhouse'. Díaz-Fernández writes of "una cueva de Robinsones". The translator asked himself the following question, what would 'Robinsons' Cave' mean to the Anglophone reader? The protagonist describes his predecessors as "ragged, bearded individuals". In order to retain the comment's original flavor, the translator rendered the sentence as "We've landed on a real Crusoe's island".

There is a back story to the onomatopoeic 'paco' and its corollary 'paqueo' which feature in 'The Blockhouse', 'Tryst in the Orchard', 'Red Magdalene', 'Death Sentence' and 'Love's Convoy'. Its significance is more than mimicry of the sound made by a bullet which the translator rendered as 'sniper' or 'sniping'. Conflict in Spain's Moroccan Protectorate often took the shape of guerrilla warfare, in which the Berbers' accurate and deadly sniping posed a constant threat taking both a physical and mental toll on the Spanish soldiery, at times reaching mythical proportions.

In the second story, 'The Pocket Watch', Díaz-Fernández relates that the soldier Villabona possessed a watch. The author tells the reader he used similes to build towards its identity, writing that it was not "un reloj de torre" but "un reloj de bolsillo". Spanish does not differentiate between 'clock' and 'watch'. It is a 'reloj' whether on a tower or in a pocket, so the process of identifying the

object in question, inevitably lost a little of its original impact in translation. The author writes that Villabona, "a simple soul" "…habia heredado el franciscanismo campesino…". The reference to the Franciscan Order proved a stout challenge, finally morphing into "had inherited the Franciscans' good nature…".

In the fourth story, 'Red Magdalene' "los barquilleros, con su caja a la espalda…" is rendered by the translator as "waffle sellers with their traditional, round, tin boxes on their backs…". Fortunately, for the reader, the Spanish waffle-selling 'barquillero', is further defined in a footnote.

Díaz Fernández writes that the 'baby' was swaying on Angustia's "… pecho intacto…"; the translator opted for the somewhat unusual "milk-less breasts". The author contrasts the fraudulent image of the 'newborn' doll with the woman who never wished to bring children into a corrupt world. This implicit message is reinforced when Angustias produces a box of matches from her cleavage, a metaphorical harbinger of death.

As the troop train pulls out from the railroad station we read that Sergeant Arnedo spent a long time at the window "recluido en el camarote de mis gafas". The noun 'Camarote' can be variously translated as 'cabin', 'car', 'coach', 'compartment'. As the protagonist's view is constricted, the translator rendered this as "imprisoned in my spectacles' narrow view".

In the same story, Angustias's name is dramatically stifled in the protagonist's throat becoming 'Angus'. Not unnaturally, the translator rendered this as 'Angust'.

The seventh story 'Love's Convoy' weaves erotically across the pages, presenting the translator with a number of challenges - not least when Carmen/Carmela says she would like to "Take off all these sweaty clothes and…" "Tirar toda esta ropa que llevo empapada y...". The sentence ends: "tostarme al sol", but neither 'toast in the sun', nor the modern-sounding 'sunbathe', seemed quite appropriate; the slightly more flirtatious "bathe in the sun", served to cover the situation.

Linguistic or contextual ambivalence, as the reader will appreciate, does not always transfer easily from one language to another. In preserving the depth and multiplicity of meanings of Díaz-Fernández's narrative it often required the translation to remain faithful to both the spirit and the literal articulation of the story. It was a task that could only be resolved by working through numerous drafts. We believe, however, that this translation has succeeded in preserving some of the revolutionary and highly experimental spirit that inspired Díaz-Fernández's work.

Paul Southern

BIBLIOGRAPHY

Works by José Díaz-Fernández

Arderíus, J. and Díaz-Fernández, J. 1931. *Vida de Fermín Galán (biografía política)*. Madrid: Editorial Zeus.

Díaz-Fernández, J. 1929. *La venus mecánica: Novela*. Madrid: Renacimiento.

Díaz-Fernández, J. 1930. *El nuevo romanticismo: Polémica de arte, política y literatura*. Madrid: Editorial Zeus.

Díaz-Fernández, J. 1931. 'La largueza'. *Las siete virtudes*. Ed. Antonio Espina *et al.* Madrid: Espasa-Calpe.

Díaz-Fernández, J. 1935. *Octubre rojo en Asturias: Historia de la revolución*. Madrid: Agencia General de Librería y Artes Gráficas.

Díaz-Fernández, J. 1976. *El blocao*. Ed. V. Fuentes. Madrid: Turner.

Díaz-Fernández, J. 2004. *Crónicas de la guerra de Marruecos (1921–1922)*. Ed. J. Ramón González. Gijón: Ateneo Obrero de Gijón.

Díaz-Fernández, J. 2004. *El ídolo roto y otros relatos*. Oviedo: López & Malgor.

General Bibliography on José Díaz-Fernández's Work

Álvarez, J. E. 2001. *The Betrothed of Death. The Spanish Foreign Legion During the Rif Rebellion, 1920–1927*. Westport: Greenwood Press.

Aguado, T. 2004. '*Imán*, *La ruta* y *El blocao*: Memoria e historia del desastre de Annual'. *Revista Hispánica Moderna: Boletín Del Instituto De Las Españas* 57.1, 99.

Arias-Anglés, E. 2007. 'La visión de Marruecos a través de la pintura orientalista española'. *Mélanges De La Casa De Velazquez / Casa De Velázquez*, 13–37.

Aziza, M. 2003. *La sociedad rifeña frente al Protectorado español de Marruecos (1912–1956)*. Barcelona: Edicions Bellaterra.

Bachoud, A. 1988. *Los españoles ante las campañas de Marruecos*. Madrid: Espasa Calpe.

Balfour, S. 2002. *Deadly Embrace: Morocco and the Road to the Spanish Civil War*. Oxford: Oxford University Press.

Berghaus, G. 2009. *Futurism and the Technological Imagination*. Amsterdam: Rodopi.

Bidwell, R. L. 1973. *Morocco under Colonial Rule: French Administration of Tribal Areas 1912–1956*. London: Cass.

Boahen, A. A. 1985. *Africa Under Colonial Domination 1880–1935*. London: Heinemann.

Bibliography

15

Boetsch, L. 1985. *José Díaz Fernández y la otra generación del 27*. Madrid: Pliegos.
Boetsch, L. 1986. 'La humanización de la novela de vanguardia: *El blocao* de José Díaz Fernández'. *Prosa hispánica de vanguardia*. Ed. F. Burgos. Madrid: Orígenes, 219–25.
Boetsch, L. 1997. 'Una aventura de la otra generación de 1927: Díaz Fernández, Arconada y la literatura de avanzada'. *Bazar* 4, 144–9.
Boetsch, L. 1998. 'José Ortega y Gasset en *El nuevo romanticismo* de José Díaz Fernández'. *Ramón J. Sender y sus coetáneos: homenaje a Charles L. King*. Eds M. Schneider and M. S. Vásquez. Huesca: Instituto de Estudios Altoaragoneses, 21–35.
Booth, M. 2004. *Cannabis: A History*. New York: Thomas Dunne Books/St Martin's Press.
Bordons, T. 1993. 'De la mujer moderna a la mujer nueva: *La venus mecánica* de José Díaz Fernández'. *España Contemporánea* 6.2, 19–40.
Bukharin, N. I. 1915. *Imperialism and world economy*. London: Lawrence.
Bukharin, N. I. 1924. 'Der Imperialismus und die Akkumulation des Kapitals'. *Unter dem Banner des Marxismus* 8/9: n.p..
Burke, E. 1976. *Prelude to Protectorate in Morocco: Precolonial Protest and Resistance, 1860–1912*. Chicago: University of Chicago Press.
Cardona, G. 1983. *El poder militar en la España contemporánea hasta la Guerra Civil*. Madrid: Siglo Veintiuno.
Chaney, L. 2011. *Coco Chanel: An Intimate Life*. New York: Viking.
Charnon-Deutsch, L. 2008. *Hold that Pose: Visual Culture in the Late-Nineteenth-Century Spanish Periodical*. University Park: Pennsylvania State University Press.
Clay, C. 2007. *King, Kaiser, Tsar: three royal cousins who led the world to war*. New York: Walker & Co.
Conrad, S. 2012. *German Colonialism: A Short History*. Cambridge: Cambridge University Press.
Darío, R. 1904. *Tierras solares*. Madrid: Leonardo Williams.
Dennis, N. 2010. 'José Díaz Fernández: Eroticism and Politics in the Spanish Avant-Garde'. *Journal of Iberian and Latin American Studies* 16.1, 23–34.
Derrick, J. 2008. *Africa's 'Agitators': Militant Anti-colonialism in Africa and the West, 1918–1939*. New York: Columbia University Press.
Deshen, S. A. 1989. *The Mellah Society: Jewish Community Life in Sherifian Morocco*. Chicago: University of Chicago Press.
De Torre, G. 1965. *Historia de las literaturas de vanguardia*. Madrid: Ediciones Guadarrama.
Díaz Freire, J. J. 1989. 'El progreso de las ideas: José Díaz Fernández en *El Liberal* de 1931 a 1937'. *Historia Contemporánea* 2, 267–96.
España, A. 1954. *La pequeña historia de Tánger: impresiones, recuerdos y anécdotas de una ciudad*. Tánger: Distribuciones Ibérica.
Espina, A. 1930. 'José Díaz Fernández. *El nuevo romanticismo*'. *Revista de Occidente* XXX, 374–8.

Ferragut, J. 1921. *La misma sangre: Novela de la guerra*. Madrid: Prensa Gráfica.

Ferragut, J. 1921. 'Memorias de un legionario'. *Nuevo mundo* vol. 28, issue no. 1441.

Forbes, R. 1924. *El Raisuni, the Sultan of the Mountains: His Life Story*. London: Thornton.

Fuentes, V. 1969. 'De la literatura de vanguardia a la de avanzada: en torno a José Díaz Fernández'. *Papeles de Son Armadans* 54, 243–60.

Fuentes, V. 1976. '*Post-Guerra* (1927–1928), una revista de vanguardia política y literaria'. *Ínsula* 360, 4.

Fuentes, V. 1980. 'Narrativa de 'avanzada': Arderíus, Díaz-Fernández, Sender'. *La marcha al pueblo en las letras españolas (1917–1936)*. Madrid: Ediciones de la Torre, 75–94.

Fuentes, V. 1987. 'Vanguardia, cannabis y pueblo en Valle-Inclán.' *Genio y virtuosismo de Valle-Inclán*. Ed. J. P. Garbriele. Madrid: Orígenes, 173–182.

Giménez-Caballero, E. 1923. *Notas marruecas de un soldado*. Madrid: Librería F. Beltrán.

Gómez, M. A. 2005. 'Feminismo y anarquismo. El papel de las mujeres libres en la Guerra Civil española'. Ed. L. Vollendorf. *Literatura y feminismo en España, S. XV–XXI*. Barcelona: Icaria Editorial, 267–84.

Goytisolo, J. 1989. *Crónicas sarracinas*. Barcelona: Seix Barral.

Harris, W. 1970. *Morocco That Was*. Westport: Negro Universities Press.

Hayes, C. J. H. 1941. *A Generation of materialism: 1871–1900*. New York: Harper Brothers.

Hernández, C. 1980. *Historia de las armas cortas*. León: Nebrija.

Hernández, J. 2000. 'El truncado exilio de José Díaz Fernández'. *Sesenta años después. Las literaturas del exilio republicano de 1939*. Ed. M. Aznar Soler. Barcelona: Associació d'Idees-GEXEL, 295–304.

Herzberger, D. K. 1993. 'Representation and Transcendence: the Double Sense of Díaz Fernández's *El nuevo romanticismo*'. *Letras Peninsulares* 6.1, 83–93.

Hilferding, R. 1910. *Das Finanzkapital*. Vienna: Brand.

Hobson, J. A. 1902. *Imperialism: a study*. London: Nisbet.

Hoyos, A. 1922. *Bajo el sol enemigo: Novela de la guerra*. Madrid: Prensa Gráfica

Jameson, F. 1990. 'Modernism and Imperialism'. Eds T. Eagleton, F. Jameson, E. W. Said and S. Deane. *Nationalism, Colonialism, and Literature*. Minneapolis: University of Minnesota Press, 43–68.

Jensen, G. 2005. *Franco: Soldier, Commander, Dictator*. Washington, DC: Potomac Books.

Kugler, E. 2012. *Sway of the Ottoman Empire on English Identity in the Long Eighteenth Century*. Leiden: Brill.

Larson, S. 2002. 'The Commodification of the Image of Spain's "New Woman" by Mass Culture and the Avant Garde in José Díaz Fernández's *La venus mecánica*'. *¡Agítese bien! A New Look at the Hispanic Avant-Gardes*. Ed. M. T. Pao and R. Hernández-Rodríguez. Newark: Juan de la Cuesta, 275–306.

Laskier, M. 1983. *The Alliance Israélite Universelle and the Jewish Communities of Morocco, 1862–1962.* Albany: State University of New York Press.

Lenin, V. [1916] 1963. "Imperialism, the Highest Stage of Capitalism." *Selected Works.* Moscow: Progress Publishers.

Limoncelli, S. A. 2010. *The Politics of Trafficking: The First International Movement to Combat the Sexual Exploitation of Women.* Stanford: Stanford University Press.

López de Abiada, J. M. 1980. *José Díaz Fernández: Narrador, crítico, periodista y político.* Bellinzona: Casagrande.

López de Abiada, J. M. 1982. 'José Díaz Fernández: la superación del vanguardismo'. *Los Cuadernos del Norte* 11, 56–65.

López de Abiada, J. M. 1989. 'De la literatura de vanguardia a la de avanzada. Los escritores del 27 entre la 'deshumanización' y el compromiso'. *Journal of Interdisciplinary Literary Studies* 1, 19–62.

Luxemburg, R. 1913. *Die Akkumulation des Kapitals.* Berlin: Vorwärts.

Luxemburg, R. 1915. *The Junius Pamphlet: the crisis in the German social democracy.* London: Merlin Press.

Madariaga, M. R. 2013. *Marruecos, ese gran desconocido: Breve historia del protectorado español.* Madrid: Alianza.

Martin-Marquez, S. 2008. *Disorientations.* New Haven: Yale University Press.

Masjuan-Bracons, E. 2000. *La ecología humana en el anarquismo ibérico: urbanismo 'orgánico' o ecológico, neomalthusianismo y naturismo social.* Barcelona: Icaria.

Meaker, G. H. 1974. *The Revolutionary Left in Spain, 1914–1923.* Stanford: Stanford University Press.

Micó-España, C. 1922. *El camillero de la legión. Novela de la guerra.* Madrid: Sucesores de Rivadeneyra.

Micó-España, C. 1922. *Lupo, sargento: Novela de la guerra.* Madrid: Hermosilla, 1922.

Miranda Calvo, J. 1996. 'Toledo en la obra musical de Jacinto Guerrero'. *Toletum.* 34, 87–101.

Nerín, G. 2005. *La guerra que vino de África.* Barcelona: Crítica.

Nerín, G. 1998. *Guinea Ecuatorial: historia en blanco y negro: hombres blancos y mujeres negras en Guinea Ecuatorial, 1843–1968.* Barcelona: Península.

Payne, S. G. 1967. *Politics and the Military in Modern Spain.* Stanford: Stanford University Press.

Perdicaris, I. 1906. 'Morocco. The Land of the Extreme West'. *National Geographic* XVII.3, 117–57.

Picasso, G. J. 1976. *Expediente Picasso: documentos relacionados con la información instruida por el señor General de División D. Juan Picasso sobre las responsabilidades de la actuación española en Marruecos durante julio de mil novecientos veintiuno.* México: Frente de Afirmación Hispanista.

Pitts, J. 2005. *A Turn to Empire: the Rise of Imperial Liberalism in Britain and France.* Princeton: Princeton University Press.

Preston, P. 1994. *The Spanish Civil War: Reform, Reaction, and Revolution in the Second Republic.* London: Routledge.

Purkey, L. C. 2013a. *Spanish Reception of Russian Narratives, 1905–1939: Transcultural Dialogues.* Woodbridge: Tamesis.

Purkey, L. C. 2013b. 'Nuevo romanticismo and Futurism: Spanish Responses to Machine Culture'. *International Yearbook of Futurism Studies,* 181–207.

Röhl, J. C. G. 2014. *Kaiser Wilhelm II: A Concise Life.* Cambridge: Cambridge University Press.

Santonja, G. 1986. *Del lápiz rojo al lápiz libre: la censura previa de publicaciones periódicas y sus consecuencias editoriales durante los últimos años del reinado de Alfonso XIII.* Barcelona: Anthropos Editorial del Hombre.

Schneider, Marshall J. 1994. 'Toward a New Vanguard: Ideology and Novelistic Form in José Díaz Fernández's *El blocao'. Hispania* 77.3, 406–15.

Schneider, M. J. 1998. 'The Genealogy and Praxis of New Romanticism: From the Nineteenth Century to the New Vanguard'. *Ramón J. Sender y sus coetáneos: Homenaje a Charles L. King.* Eds M. Schneider and M. S. Vásquez. Huesca: Instituto de Estudios Altoaragoneses, 63–81.

Tiffin, H. 1995. 'Post-colonial Literatures and Counter-Discourse'. *The Post-colonial Studies Reader.* Eds B. Ashcroft, G. Griffiths and H. Tiffin. *London: Routledge.*

Valle-Inclán, R. del. 1919. *La Pipa de Kif, versos.* Madrid: Sociedad General Española de Librería.

Vicente-Hernando, C. 2013. *Una generación perdida: El tiempo de la literatura de avanzada (1925–1935).* Doral: Stock Cero.

Vicente-Hernando, C. 1993. 'Representaciones sociales de la vanguardia: *La venus mecánica* y *Metrópolis'. Letras Peninsulares* 6.1, 109–25.

Vilches de Frutos, M. F. 1984. *La generación del nuevo romanticismo: Estudio bibliográfico y crítico (1924–1939).* Madrid: Editorial de la Universidad Complutense.

Wilhelm II. 1922. *The Kaiser's memoirs, Wilhelm II, emperor of Germany, 1888–1918*; English translation by Thomas R. Ybarra. New York: Harper.

Wrigley, C. 2002. *Challenges of Labour: Central and Western Europe, 1917–1920.* London: Routledge.

THE BLOCKHOUSE
A NOVEL OF THE MORROCAN WAR

EL BLOCAO
NOVELA DE LA GUERRA MARROQUÍ

DEDICATORIA

Este libro está escrito sobre una falsilla de recuerdos. El autor ha preferido para los seis relatos un estilo recto y desnudo, donde la economía verbal favorezca a la emoción. Si el autor se sintiese militante de una estética, quizás la resumiera en dos palabras: emoción, síntesis. Pero se trata de una obra demasiado personal para que pretenda el valor de la objetividad. Intenta solamente extraer de entre el légamo de la memoria impresiones que quizás resuenen todavía en la intimidad de algunas almas. Aunque otra cosa se diga, Marruecos sigue siendo una herida abierta en la conciencia española. A los espíritus civiles de aquellos soldados que fueron compañeros suyos en el Marruecos de 1921, dedica el autor este libro.

DEDICATION

This book is written on a framework of recollections. The author has preferred an unadorned style for the six stories, in which verbal economy favors emotion. If the author were a militant of an esthetic, then perhaps it could be summarised in two words: emotion, synthesis. However, this is a much too personal work to be objective. It merely seeks to extract impressions from memory's clay that perhaps still resound in the intimacy of some souls. Even if the opposite is said, Morocco continues to be an open wound in the Spanish consciousness. The author dedicates this book to the civilian spirit of those soldiers who were his comrades in Morocco in 1921.

1

EL BLOCAO

Llevábamos cinco meses en aquel blocao y no teníamos esperanzas de relevo. Nuestros antecesores habían guarnecido la posición año y medio. Los recuerdo feroces y barbudos, con sus uniformes desgarrados, mirando de reojo, con cierto rencor, nuestros rostros limpios y sonrientes. Yo le dije a Pedro Núñez, el cabo:

–Hemos caído en una cueva de Robinsones.

El sargento que me hizo entrega del puesto se despidió de mí con ironías como ésta:

–Buena suerte, compañero. Esto es un poco aburrido, sobre todo para un cuota. Algo así como estar vivo y metido en una caja de muerto.

«¡Qué bárbaro!», pensé. No podía comprender sus palabras. Porque entonces iba yo de Tetuán, ciudad de amor más que de guerra, y llevaba en mi hombro suspiros de las mujeres de tres razas. Los expedicionarios del 78 de Infantería no habíamos sufrido todavía la campaña ni traspasado las puertas de la ciudad. Nuestro heroísmo no había tenido ocasión de manifestarse más que escalando balcones en la Sueca, jaulas de hebreas enamoradas, y acechando las azoteas del barrio moro, por donde al atardecer jugaban las mujeres de los babucheros y los notarios. Cuando a nuestro batallón lo distribuyeron por las avanzadas de Beni Arós, y a mí me destinaron, con veinte hombres, a un blocao, yo me alegré, porque iba, al fin, a vivir la existencia difícil de la guerra.

Confieso que en aquel tiempo mi juventud era un tanto presuntuosa. No me gustaba la milicia; pero mis nervios, ante los actos que juzgaba comprometidos, eran como una traílla de perros difícil de sujetar bajo la voz del cuerno de caza. Me fastidiaban las veladas de la alcazaba, entre cante jondo y mantones de flecos, tanto como la jactancia de algunos alféreces, que hacían sonar sus cruces de guerra en el paseo nocturno de la plaza de España.

Por eso la despedida del sargento me irritó. Se lo dije a Pedro Núñez, futuro ingeniero y *goal-keeper* de un equipo de fútbol:

1

THE BLOCKHOUSE

We had been in that blockhouse[1] for five months and we had no hope of relief. Our predecessors had manned the position for a year and a half. I remember them, fierce-looking and bearded, with tattered uniforms, glancing somewhat bitterly out of the corner of their eyes at our fresh and smiling faces. I said to Pedro Núñez, the corporal:

"We've landed on a real Crusoe's island."[2]

The sergeant who handed over the post took his leave with these ironic words:

"Good luck, comrade. It's kind of boring, above all for a quota-man. It's a bit like being buried alive in a coffin."[3]

"How awful!" I thought. I did not know what his words meant. Because, coming fresh from Tetouan,[4] I brought with me the sighs of women of three races; it was a city of love, rather than of war. We, the expeditionary troops of 78th Infantry, had no experience of campaigning nor had we even gone beyond the city's gates. Until now, we had not had the chance to display our heroism, other than in scaling balconies and entering Jewish lovers' rooms in the Sueca,[5] and spying on the wives of the sandal-sellers and the scribes at play, on the terraced roofs of the Moorish quarter as evening fell. When our battalion was deployed to the front at Beni Arós, and I was detailed with twenty men to a blockhouse,I was delighted, because at last, I was going to live the harsh life of war.

I confess that at that time in my youth, I was rather full of myself. I did not like the draft at all; but my reactions, when faced with acts that I judged to be compromising, were akin to a pack of dogs straining for the hunting horn's blast. The musical evenings in the Alcazaba[6] annoyed me, with their *cante jondo*,[7] and embroidered shawls, as did the arrogance of some second lieutenants, with their clanking war crosses during evening strolls along the Plaza de España.

That is why the sergeant's leave-taking irritated me. I said to Pedro Núñez, future civil engineer and soccer team goalkeeper:

 El blocao

–Estos desgraciados creen que nos asustan. A mí me tiene sin cuidado estar aquí seis meses o dos años. Y, además, tengo ganas de andar a tiros. Pero a los quince días ya no me atrevía a hablar así. Era demasiado aburrido. Los soldados se pasaban las horas sobre las escuálidas colchonetas, jugando a los naipes. Al principio, yo quise evitarlo. Aun careciendo de espíritu militar, no me parecía razonable quebrantar de aquel modo la moral cuartelera. Pedro Núñez, que jugaba más que nadie, se puso de parte de los soldados.

–Chico –me dijo–, ¿qué vamos a hacer si no? Esto es un suplicio. Ni siquiera nos atacan.

Al fin consentí. Paseando por el estrecho recinto sentía el paso lento y penoso de los días, como un desfile de dromedarios. Yo mismo, desde mi catre, lancé un día una moneda entre la alegre estupefacción de la partida:

–Dos pesetas a ese as.

Las perdí, por cierto. Los haberes del destacamento aumentaban cada semana, a medida que llegaban los convoyes; pero iban íntegros de un jugador a otro, según variaba la suerte. Aquello me dio, por primera vez, una idea aproximada de la economía social. Había un soldado vasco que ganaba siempre; pero como hacía préstamos a los restantes, el desequilibrio del azar desaparecía. Pensé entonces que en toda república bien ordenada el prestamista es insustituible. Pero pensé también en la necesidad de engañarle.

El juego no bastaba, sin embargo. Cada día éramos más un rebaño de bestezuelas resignadas en el refugio de una colina. Poco a poco, los soldados se iban olvidando de retozar entre sí, y ya era raro oír allí dentro el cohete de una risa. Llegaba a inquietarme la actitud inmóvil de los centinelas tras la herida de piedra de las aspilleras, porque pensaba en la insurrección de aquellas almas jóvenes recluidas durante meses enteros en unos metros cuadrados de barraca. Cuando llegaban los convoyes, yo tenía que vigilar más los paquetes de correo que los envoltorios de víveres. Los soldados se abalanzaban, hambrientos, sobre mi mano, que empuñaba cartas y periódicos.

–Tienes gesto de domador que reparte comida a los chacales –me decía Pedro Núñez.

Los chacales se humanizaban enseguida con una carta o un rollo de periódicos, devorados después con avidez en un rincón. Los que no recibían correspondencia me miraban recelosamente y escarbaban con los ojos mis periódicos. Tenía que prometerles una revista o un diario para calmar un poco su impaciencia.

"These wretches think they're frightening us. Personally, I'm not bothered if I'm here six months or two years. And anyway, I'm looking forward to some action."

But after just two weeks, I did not dare talk like that anymore. It was so boring. The men whiled away the hours on squalid mats, playing cards. In the beginning, I tried to avoid it. Even though I lacked military fiber, it did not seem reasonable to undermine the morale of the blockhouse in that way. Pedro Núñez, who played more than anyone, sided with the soldiers.

"Man" he said to me, "what else are we going to do? This is torture. They don't even attack us."

In the end, I gave in. Walking around the narrow compound, I felt the slow and painful passage of days like a parade of dromedaries. One day, to the cheerful astonishment of the card school, I actually tossed in a coin from my camp bed.

"Two pesetas on that ace."

Of course, I lost it. The blockhouse's pot increased weekly with the arrival of the convoys; but the pot went from one player to another, as fate dictated. For the first time it gave me a rough idea of social economy. There was a Basque soldier who always won; but because he loaned money to the others, the destabilising element of luck vanished. It then occurred to me that in all well-ordered republics the money-lender is irreplaceable. But I also thought about the need to cheat him.

Playing cards certainly was not enough. Every day we became more like beasts resigned in the shelter of a hill. Little by little, the soldiers were losing their sense of fun, and it was unusual to hear a peel of laughter. The immobile sentries behind the loopholes of wounded stone began to worry me; it made me think about the possible insubordination of those young souls holed up for months at a time within the hut's scant square meters. When the convoys arrived, I had to keep more of an eye on the mail bags than on the packs of rations. The soldiers hungrily pounced on my hand as I clutched letters and newspapers.

"You've got the look of a trainer feeding jackals," Pedro Núñez said to me.

The jackals were quickly humanized with a letter or a bundle of newspapers, avidly devoured in a corner. Those who did not receive letters looked at me suspiciously as their eyes pried into my newspapers. I had to promise them a magazine or a daily paper to calm their impatience a little.

Sin darnos cuenta, cada día nos parecíamos más a aquellos peludos a quienes habíamos sustituido. Éramos como una reproducción de ellos mismos, y nuestra semejanza era una semejanza de cadáveres verticales movidos por un oscuro mecanismo. El enemigo no estaba abajo, en la cabila, que parecía una vedija verde entre las calaveras mondadas de dos lomas. El enemigo andaba por entre nosotros, calzado de silencio, envuelto en el velo impalpable del fastidio.

Alguna noche, el proyectil de un paco venía a clavarse en el parapeto. Lo recibíamos con júbilo, como una llamada alegre de tambor, esperando un ataque que hiciera cambiar, aunque fuera trágicamente, nuestra suerte. Pero no pasaba de ahí. Yo distribuía a los soldados por las troneras y me complacía en darles órdenes para una supuesta lucha, una lucha que no llegaba nunca. Dijérase que los moros preferían para nosotros el martirio de la monotonía. A las dos horas de esperarlos, yo me cansaba, y, lleno de rabia, mandaba hacer una descarga cerrada.

Como si quisiera herir, en su vientre sombrío, a la tranquila noche marroquí.

Un domingo se me puso enfermo un soldado. Era rubio y tímido y hablaba siempre en voz baja. Tenía el oficio de aserrador en su montaña gallega. Una tarde, paseando por el recinto, me había hablado de su oficio, de su larga sierra que mutilaba castaños y abedules, del rocío dorado de la madera, que le caía sobre los hombros como un manto. El cabo y yo vimos cómo el termómetro señalaba horas después los 40 grados. En la bolsa de curación no había más que quinina, y le dimos quinina.

Al día siguiente, la fiebre alta continuaba. Era en febrero y llovía mucho. No podíamos, pues, utilizar el heliógrafo para avisar al campamento general. En vano hice funcionar el telégrafo de banderas. Faltaban cinco días para la llegada del convoy, y yo temía que el soldado se me muriese allí, sobre mi catre, entre la niebla del delirio.

Me pasaba las horas en la explanada del blocao, buscando entre la espesura de las nubes un poco de sol para mis espejos. En vano sangraban en mis manos las banderas de señales. Pedíamos al cielo un resplandor, un guiño de luz para salvar una vida.

Pero el soldado, en sus momentos de lucidez, sonreía. Sonreía porque Pedro Núñez le anunciaba:

–Pronto te llevarán al hospital.

Otro soldado subrayaba, con envidia:

–¡Al hospital! Allí sí que se está bien.

Without realizing it, with every day we began to look more like that hairy bunch we had replaced. We were like a reproduction of their very selves, and the likeness was a likeness of vertical corpses moved by a dark mechanism. The enemy was not below in its village which looked like a tuft of green wool between the bare skulls of the hills. The enemy walked among us, shod with silence, wrapped in an imperceptible, tiresome veil.

One night, a sniper's bullet lodged itself in the parapet. We greeted it with joy, like the cheerful call of the drum, expecting an attack that could, even if tragically, change our fate. But nothing came of it. I allocated loopholes to the men and it cheered me to be giving them orders for a possible fight. A fight that never happened. It was said that the Moors preferred us to suffer the martyrdom of monotony. After two hours of waiting for them, I got fed up, and, full of anger, I ordered volley fire.

As if to wound the dark womb of the peaceful Moroccan night.

One Sunday a soldier fell ill on me. He was fair-haired and shy and always softly spoken. He was a woodcutter on his Galician mountain. One evening, walking through the compound, he had talked to me about his job, about his large saw which mutilated chestnut and silver birch trees, and of the forest's golden sap which settled on his shoulders like a cloak. Hours later the corporal and I saw the thermometer was showing 40 degrees centigrade. There was only quinine in the medical kit, and we gave him quinine.

He still had a high fever the next day. It was February and it rained a lot, so we could not use the heliograph to alert the base camp. In vain I tried to signal by semaphore. The convoy was due to arrive in five days, and I was afraid that the soldier would die on me, on my camp-bed, there between the mist of delirium.

I spent hours on the open ground by the blockhouse, with my mirrors looking for a little sun between the thick clouds. I bloodied my hands in vain with the signal flags. We begged the sky for sunlight; a blink of light to save a life.

But the soldier, in his lucid moments, smiled. He smiled because Pedro Núñez told him:

"They'll soon take you to the hospital."

Another soldier said with an emphasis redolent of envy:

"The hospital! You'll be just fine there."

Preferían la enfermedad; yo creo que preferían la muerte.
Por fin, el jueves, la víspera del convoy, hizo sol. Me apresuré a captarlo
en el heliógrafo y escribir con alfabeto de luz un aviso de sombras.
Por la tarde se presentó un convoy con el médico. El enfermo marchó
en una artola, sonriendo, hacia el hospital. Creo que salió de allí para el
cementerio. Pero en mi blocao no podía morir, porque, aun siendo un ataúd,
no era un ataúd de muertos.

Una mujer. Mis veintidós años vociferaban en coro la preciosa ausencia.
En mi vida había una breve biografía erótica. Pero aquella soledad del
destacamento señalaba mis amores pasados como un campo sin árboles.
Mi memoria era una puerta entreabierta por donde yo, con sigilosa
complacencia, observaba una cita, una espera, un idilio ilegal. Este hombre
voraz que va conmigo, este que conspira contra mi seriedad y me denuncia
inopinadamente cuando una mujer pasa por mi lado, era el que paseaba
su carne inútil alrededor del blocao. Por ese túnel del recuerdo llegaban
las tardes de cinematógrafo, las rutilantes noches de verbena, los alegres
mediodías de la playa. Volaban las pamelas en el viento de julio y ardían los
disfraces de un baile bajo el esmeril de la helada. Mi huésped subconsciente
colocaba a todas horas delante de mis ojos su retablo de delicias, su sensual
fantasmagoría, su implacable obsesión.

Y no era yo solo. Al atardecer, los soldados, en corro, sostenían diálogos
obscenos, que yo sorprendía al pasar, un poco avergonzado de la coincidencia.

–Porque la mujer del teniente...

–Estaba loca, loca...

Sólo la saludable juventud de Pedro Núñez se salvaba allí. Yo iba a
curarme en sus anécdotas estudiantiles, en sus nostalgias de gimnasio y
alpinismo, como un enfermo urbano que sale al aire de la sierra.

Una de mis distracciones era observar, con el anteojo de campaña, la
cabila vecina. La cabila me daba una acentuada sensación de vida en común,
de macrocosmos social, que no podía obtener del régimen militar de mi
puesto. Desde muy temprano, mi lente acechaba por el párpado abierto de
una aspillera. El aduar estaba sumergido en un barranco y tenía que esperar,
para verlo, a que el sol quemase las telas de la niebla. Entonces aparecían
allá abajo, como en las linternas mágicas de los niños, la mora del pollino y
el moro del Rémington, la chumbera y la vaca, el columpio del humo sobre
la choza gris.

They would have preferred sickness; I believe they would have preferred death.

Finally, on Thursday, the eve of the convoy, the sun came out. I rushed to capture it on the heliograph and write the somber news with an alphabet of light.

That afternoon a convoy arrived with a medic. The sick man left for the hospital riding on a wooden saddle, smiling. I believe he left there for the cemetery. But he could not die in my blockhouse, because even though it was a coffin, it was not a coffin of the dead.

A woman. All of my twenty-two years cried out for that precious absence. An erotic biography made up only a brief part of my life. But the solitude of that post displayed my past lovers like a field bereft of trees. My memory was a half-open door through which, I watched a tryst, an expectation and an illegal idyll, with stealthy pleasure. This voracious man who shadows me, he who conspires against my serious side and unexpectedly betrays me when a woman passes by, it was he who walked his useless body around the blockhouse. Through this tunnel of recollections came evenings at the picture shows, starry nights of open air dances, and happy middays on the beach. Girls' large, straw hats flying off in the July winds, and flaming dresses at dances under the sparkled dusting of early morning frost. My subconscious lodger at all hours placed before my eyes a theater of delights; his sensual phantasmagoria, and his implacable obsession.

And I was not alone. At nightfall, as I walked by, I surprised all the soldiers holding lewd conversations and was a little embarrassed by the coincidence.

"Because the lieutenant's wife …"

"She was crazy, crazy …"

My only salvation there was Pedro Núñez's fresh, youthfulness. I would go and cure myself through his student anecdotes, his nostalgia for the gymnasium and for rock climbing, like a sick city-dweller, who goes out into the mountain air.

One of my distractions was to watch the nearby tribe through my field telescope. The tribe gave me a heightened sense of communal life, of social macrocosms, which could not be got through the military constraints of my position. From very early on, my lens was there, watching through the loophole's open eyelid. The Moorish village was way down in a ravine and I had to wait until the sun burnt away the threads of mist before I could see it. Then there below, like in a children's magic lantern show, the gray hut appeared through the hanging smoke, along with the Moorish girl with the donkey, the Moor with the Remington rifle, the prickly pear tree, and the cow.

Buscaba a la mujer. A veces, una silueta blanca que se evaporaba con frecuencia entre las higueras hacía fluir en mí una rara congoja, la tierna congoja del sexo. ¿Qué clase de emoción era aquélla que en medio del campo solitario me ponía en contacto con la inquietud universal? Allí me reconocía. Yo era el mismo que en una calle civilizada, entre la orquesta de los timbres y las bocinas, esperaba a la muchacha del escritorio o del *dancing*. Yo era el náufrago en el arenal de la acera, con mi alga rubia y escurridiza en el brazo, cogida en el océano de un comedor de hotel. Y aquel sufrimiento de entonces, tras el tubo del anteojo, buscando a cuatro kilómetros de distancia el lienzo tosco de una mora, era el mismo que me había turbado en la selva de una gran ciudad.

Nuestra única visita, aparte del convoy, era una mora de apenas quince años, que nos vendía higos chumbos, huevos y gallinas.

–¿Cómo te llamas, morita?

–Aixa.

Era delgada y menuda, con piernas de galgo. Lo único que tenía hermoso era la boca. Una boca grande, frutal y alegre, siempre con la almendra de una sonrisa entre los labios.

–¡Paisa! ¡Paisa!

Chillaba como un pajarraco cuando, al verla, la tromba de soldados se derrumbaba sobre la alambrada. Yo tenía que detenerlos:

–¡Atrás! ¡Atrás! Todo el mundo adentro.

Ella entonces sacaba de entre la paja de la canasta los huevos y los higos y me los ofrecía en su mano sucia y dura. Yo, en broma, le iba enseñando monedas de cobre; pero ella las rechazaba con un mohín hasta que veía brillar las piezas de plata. A veces, se me quedaba mirando con fijeza, y a mí me parecía ver en aquellos ojos el brillo de un reptil en el fondo de la noche. Pero en alguna ocasión el contacto con la piel áspera de su mano me enardecía, y cierta furia sensual desesperaba mis nervios. Entonces la dejaba marchar y le volvía la espalda para desengancharme definitivamente de su mirada.

Un anochecer, cuando ya habíamos cerrado la alambrada, Pedro Núñez vino a avisarme:

–El centinela dice que ahí está la morita.

–¡A estas horas!

–Yo creo que debemos decirle que se vaya. Porque esta gente…

–¿No ha dicho qué quiere?

–Ha pedido que te avise.

I was looking for women. At times, a white silhouette would evaporate between the fig trees; then a strange anguish flowed through me, the tender anguish of sex. What type of emotion was that which in the midst of a lonely countryside put me in contact with that universal disquiet? I saw myself there. I was the same person who in a civilized street, among the orchestra of bells and horns, would wait for the young woman from the office or the dance hall. I was the shipwrecked sailor on the sidewalk strand, with my blonde and slippery seaweed on my arm, caught in the ocean of a hotel dining room. And that suffering then, through the telescope's tube, searching at a distance of four kilometers for the Moorish girl's coarse garb, was the same as that which had troubled me in the jungle of a great city.

Our only visitor, apart from the convoy, was a Moorish girl, hardly fifteen years old, who sold us prickly pears, eggs and chickens.[8]

"What's your name, little Moor?"

"Aisha."

She was small and slim, with legs like a greyhound. The only attractive thing about her was her mouth. A big, fruity and happy mouth, she always had the almond of a smile between her lips.

"Friend! Friend!"

The men caught sight of her and in a whirlwind, tumbled down against the barbed wire, all the while she was screeching like an ugly bird. I had to stop them:

"Back! Back! Everybody inside."

Then she would produce eggs and figs from under the straw in her basket, and offer them to me in her hard and dirty hand. As a joke, I would show her my copper coins; but she would refuse them by making a face until she saw the shiny pieces of silver. At times, when she stared intently into my eyes, I seemed to see a reptilian sheen from the depths of the night. But at other times, contact with her rough-skinned hands would inflame me, and a certain, sensual fury would grip my nerves. Then I would let her go and turn my back to free myself completely from her gaze.[9]

One night, when we had already closed the barbed wire fence, Pedro Núñez came to warn me:

"The sentry reports that the little Moorish girl is there."

"At this hour!"

"I think we ought to tell her to go away. Because these people …"

"Did she not say what she wants?"

"He asked me to report it to you."

–Voy a ver.

–No salgas, ¿eh? Sería una imprudencia.

–¡Bah! Tendrá falta de dinero.

Salí al recinto. Aixa estaba allí, tras los alambres, sonriente, con su canasta en la mano.

–¿Qué quieres tú a estas horas?

–¡Paisa! Higos.

–No es hora de traerlos.

Le vi un gesto, entre desolado y humilde, que me enterneció. Y sentí como nunca un urgente deseo de mujer, una oscura y voluptuosa desazón. La figura blanca de Aixa estaba como suspendida entre las últimas luces de la tarde y las primeras sombras de la noche. Abrí la alambrada.

–Vamos a ver qué traes.

Aixa dio un grito, no sé si de dolor o de júbilo. Y aquello fue tan rápido que las frases más concisas son demasiado largas para contarlo. Un centinela gritó:

–¡Mi sargento, los moros!

Sonó una descarga a mi izquierda en el momento en que yo me tiraba al suelo, sujetando a la mora por las ropas. La arrastré de un tirón hasta las puertas del blocao, y allí me hirieron. Pedro Núñez nos recogió a los dos cuando ya los moros saltaban la alambrada chillando y haciendo fuego. Fue una lucha a muerte, una lucha de cuatro horas, donde el enemigo llegaba a meter sus fusiles por las aspilleras. Pero eran pocos, no más de cincuenta. Yo mismo até a Aixa y la arrojé a un rincón, mientras Pedro Núñez disponía la defensa.

No me dolía la herida y pude estar mucho tiempo haciendo fuego en el puesto de un soldado muerto.

A medianoche los moros se retiraron. Al parecer, tenían pocas municiones y habían querido ganarnos por sorpresa. Pedro Núñez me vendó cuando ya me faltaban las fuerzas. Había cuatro soldados muertos y otros tres heridos. Casi nos habíamos olvidado de Aixa, que permanecía en un rincón, prisionera. Me acerqué a ella, y a la luz de una cerilla vi sus ojos fríos y tranquilos. Ya no tenía en la boca su sonrisa de almendra. Me dieron ganas de matarla yo mismo allí dentro. Pero llamé a los soldados:

–Que nadie la toque. Es una prisionera y hay que tratarla bien.

Al día siguiente, cuando ya habíamos transmitido al campamento general la noticia del ataque, llamé a Pedro Núñez:

"I'll go and see."

"Listen, don't go, eh? It might be risky."

"Oh! She's just short of money."

I went out into the compound. Aisha was there, beyond the barbed wire, smiling, with her basket in her hand.

"What do you want at this hour?"

"Friend! Figs."

"This isn't the time to bring them."

I saw her make a gesture, between desolation and humility, which moved me. And I felt as never before, the urgent desire for a woman, a dark and voluptuous unease. Aisha's white figure appeared suspended between the last light of the day and the first shadows of the night. I pulled back the barbed wire.

"Let's see what you've brought."

Aisha cried out, and I do not know if it was from pain or joy. And it was so fast that the crispest sentences would be too lengthy to describe it. A sentry shouted:

"Sergeant, Moors!"

A shot rang out to my left just as I threw myself down, holding the Moorish girl by her clothes. I dragged her with one motion towards the blockhouse doors, and that is where I was wounded. Pedro Núñez rescued us both when the Moors were already over the barbed wire shrieking and firing. It was a fight to the death, a fight that lasted four hours in which the enemy got close enough to stick their rifles through the loopholes. But there were few of them, not more than fifty. I tied up Aisha myself and threw her in a corner, while Pedro Núñez organized the defenses.

My wound did not hurt me and I managed to carry on for ages, firing from a dead soldier's position.

The Moors withdrew at midnight. Apparently, they had little ammunition and had wanted to take us by surprise. Pedro Núñez bandaged me when I no longer had the strength. Four soldiers were dead and another three wounded. We had almost forgotten about Aisha, who was still in the corner, a prisoner. I went up to her, and by the light of a match I saw her cold and calm eyes. She no longer had that almond smile on her lips. I wanted to kill her myself, there and then. But I called the men together:

"Don't anybody touch her. She's a prisoner and has to be well treated."

Next day, when we had already transmitted the news of the attack to base camp, I called for Pedro Núñez.

–Debo de tener fiebre.

–Efectivamente, 39 y décimas.

–¿Y la mora?

–Ahí está; como si no hubiera hecho nada. ¿Qué vamos a hacer con ella? Me encogí de hombros. Yo mismo no lo sabía.

–Debíamos fusilarla –dije yo sin gran convencimiento.

–Eso dicen los soldados. Toda la noche han estado hablando de matarla. Yo pensé en aquellos quince años malignos, en aquella sonrisa dulce; pero también pensé en aquel heroísmo grandioso y único.

–Ayudó a los suyos.

Pedro Núñez se enfadó:

–¿Todavía la defiendes? ¿Hay derecho a eso?

–¡Yo qué sé! Tráela aquí.

Vino maniatada y me miró con aire indiferente. Tuve un acceso de rabia y la insulté, la maldije, quise tirarle a la cabeza un paquete de periódicos. Pero volví a quedarme silencioso, con el recuerdo sensual de la víspera, que esta vez caía en mi conciencia como una piedra en una superficie de cristal.

–¿Y qué conseguimos con que muera, Pedro?

–Castigarla, dar ejemplo.

–¡Una niña de quince años!

–No paga con la muerte. Ahí tienes cuatro soldados que mató ella. Yo se la entregaré al capitán.

Tuvimos una larga disputa. Por fin, Pedro Núñez me amenazó:

–Si tú la pones en libertad, tú sufrirás las consecuencias.

–Yo soy el jefe. A ver, ¡desátala!

Pedro Núñez, pálido, la desató. Yo me levanté trabajosamente y la cogí de un brazo.

–¡Fuera! ¡A tu cabila!

Entre los soldados que presenciaban la escena se levantó un murmullo. Me volví hacia ellos:

–¿Quién es el que protesta? ¿Quién manda aquí?

Callaron. Empujé a la mora hacia la puerta, y ella me miró despacio, con la misma frialdad. A pasos lentos salió del blocao. La vi marchar, sin prisa y sin volver la cabeza, por el camino de la cabila.

Entonces yo me tumbé sobre el camastro. Me dolía mucho mi herida.

"I must have a fever."

"You do – 39 and a bit."

"And the Moorish girl?"

"She's over there; looking as though she hadn't done anything. What are we going to do with her?"

I shrugged my shoulders. I did not know myself.

"We ought to shoot her" I said without great conviction.

"That's what the men say. They've been talking all night about killing her."

I thought about those malignant fifteen years, about that sweet smile; but I also thought about her amazing and remarkable heroism.

"She was helping her own."

Pedro Núñez got angry.

"Are you still sticking up for her? Is that fair?"

"How should I know? Bring her here."

She came with hands tied and looked at me with an air of indifference. In a burst of rage, I insulted her, cursed her and felt like throwing a bundle of newspapers at her head. But I quietened down, as the sensual recollections of the day before now weighed on my conscience like a stone hitting a glassy surface.

"And what do we achieve by her death Pedro?"

"Punish her, set an example."

"She's a fifteen-year-old kid!"

"She won't pay with her life. There are four soldiers over there that she killed. I'm going to hand her over to the captain."

We had a long argument. Finally, Pedro Núñez threatened me:

"If you free her, you'll suffer the consequences."

"I'm in command. Right, untie her!"

An ashen Pedro Núñez untied her. I got up with difficulty and grabbed her by the arm.

"Get out! Go back to your tribe!"

A murmur arose among the watching soldiers. I turned to face them:

"Who's grumbling? Who's in charge here?"

They fell silent. I pushed the Moorish girl towards the door and she looked at me deliberately, with that same coldness. She slowly made her way out of the blockhouse. I watched her walk along the road home, unhurried, never turning her head.

I then fell onto the camp-bed. I felt the pain of my wound.

2

EL RELOJ

Hay almas tan sencillas que son las únicas capaces de comprender la vida de las cosas. Eso es algo más difícil que la teoría einsteiniana.

Villabona, el de Arroes, poseía un reloj que era el asombro de la compañía; uno de esos cronómetros ingentes que hace años fabricaban los alemanes para demostrar que la Alemania del Káiser era grande en todo. Ojo de cíclope, rueda de tren, cebolla de acero. Como ya entonces sentía yo aficiones literarias, recuerdo que utilizaba esos símiles para designar aquel ejemplar único de reloj. Pero, a pesar de tales dimensiones, no era un reloj de torre, sino un reloj de bolsillo. De bolsillo, claro está, como los que usaba Villabona, especie de alforjas en el interior del pantalón, cuyo volumen producía verdadera ira a los sargentos de semana.

Pero antes de contar la historia del reloj de Villabona, oídme una breve biografía de Villabona.

Le conocí en el cuartel, a los pocos días de nuestra incorporación, con motivo de la rota de Annual. Como no se había decidido a irse a América, sus padres, unos labriegos sin suerte, invirtieron el dinero del pasaje en pagarle la cuota militar. Y he aquí a Villabona, gañán de caserío, buen segador de hierba, clasificado entre los señoritos de la compañía.

Villabona recibió la orden de presentarse en el cuartel la misma mañana de su boda. Como Villabona era un ser elemental y había heredado el franciscanismo campesino, desde la iglesia se encaminó al cuartel a pie, con su paso tardo y manso. La novia quedó intacta, envuelta en su ropa de domingo, como una castaña en su cáscara morena. En la compañía, que conocía este episodio de Villabona, le interrogaban con malicia:

–¿Y pasó sola la noche, Villabona?

–Pasó.

–¡Pobre! Entonces, ¿para qué te casaste?

–Una vaca más que mantener.

–¡Qué bárbaro!

2

THE POCKET WATCH

The life of things can only be truly comprehended by the simplest of souls. This is something rather more difficult than Einstein's theory.

Villabona, the one from Arroes in Asturias, owned a watch that was the wonder of the company; it was one of those huge chronometers made many years ago by the Germans to demonstrate that the Kaiser's Germany was great in every way.[10] A Cyclops' eye, a train wheel, a steel bulb. As I already had literary inclinations, I recall that I used these similes to describe that unique example of a watch. But, in spite of such dimensions, it was not in a clock tower; rather it was a pocket watch. It certainly was for a pocket, like Villabona's, a sort of knapsack inside his pants, whose size made the duty sergeants really angry.

But before I tell the story of Villabona's pocket watch, listen to my brief biography of Villabona.

I met him in the barracks, a few days after our being drafted, due to the Disaster of Annual.[11] As he had decided not to go to America, his parents,ill-fated farm hands, decided instead to invested the fare in paying his military quota. And here is the self-same Villabona, a farm-hand and a good reaper, being classified as one of the young gentlemen of the company.

Villabona was ordered to present himself at the barracks on the very morning of his wedding. As Villabona was a simple soul and had inherited the Franciscans' good nature which one can only find among the peasantry, he went, with his slow, deliberate step, from church to barracks. His bride remained intact, dressed in her Sunday Best, like a chestnut in its dark shell. In the Company, where this episode of Villabona's was common knowledge, they would ask him maliciously:

"And did she spend the night on her own, Villabona?"

"She did."

"Poor thing! Then, why did you marry her?"

"Yet another cow to keep."

"How awful!"

El reloj de Villabona llegó a hacerse famoso en el cuartel. Venían a la nuestra soldados de todas las compañías para conocer el artefacto. Villabona se resistía a enseñarlo; pero, al fin, lo extraía del fardo de su bolsillo y lo colocaba en la palma de su mano, como una tortuga sobre una losa. El soldado espectador lo miraba con la misma prevención que se mira a un mamífero domesticado. Villabona, en cambio, sonreía; la feliz y bondadosa sonrisa podría traducirse así: «Ya ves, yo no le tengo miedo. Es muy dócil».

Pero cuando el reloj adquirió su verdadera celebridad fue en una revista, pocos días antes de que embarcásemos para Marruecos. El sargento Arango nos formó velozmente, porque siempre llegaba tarde. En el silencio de la fila el reloj de Villabona jadeaba como una vulpeja en una trampa. Pasó primero el teniente, miope, distraído, que se detuvo, sin embargo, dos o tres veces, inquiriendo aquel rumor insólito. Después vino el capitán, alto, curvado. Se puso a escuchar, sin decir nada, y se le vio unos minutos intranquilo, mirando de reojo a los rincones, hasta que llegaron juntos, disputando en alta voz, el comandante y el teniente coronel. De pronto:

—¡Compañía! ¡El coronel!

El coronel era un anciano corpulento y malhumorado. Empezó por arrestar al segundo de la fila.

—Éste no tiene bigote —dijo señalando a Pérez, un muchacho lampiño que estudiaba matemáticas.

—Es que… verá usía, mi coronel… —respondió el capitán.

—Nada, nada. He dicho que todos vayan pelados al rape y con bigote. No quiero señoras en mi regimiento. ¡Bigote! ¡Bigote!

Aquella desaforada invocación al vello producía en los restantes jefes una visible desazón. Todos miraban al pobre Pérez como a un relapso, un proscrito, un mal soldado de España. Pérez temblaba.

—Es que —se atrevió a decir el capitán— a este soldado no le sale el bigote.

—Pues al calabozo, hasta que le salga.

Después de aquella detonación verbal, el silencio era hondo y angustioso. El reloj de Villabona se oía más claro y preciso que nunca. Un escalofrío de terror recorrió la fila. El teniente coronel miraba al comandante, y el capitán al teniente.

—¿Qué es eso? ¿Hay ratas por aquí? —dijo el coronel, recorriendo el suelo con la mirada.

—Mi coronel… —balbuceó el capitán.

Villabona's pocket watch garnered fame in the barracks. Soldiers from all the other Companies came round to look at that artefact. At first Villabona refused to show it off; but in the end, he would pull it out of the bundle in his pocket and place it on the palm of his hand, like a tortoise on a flagstone. The soldier-spectator would look at it with the same caution he would reserve for a domestic mammal.[12] Villabona, on the other hand, would smile; that happy and friendly smile could be translated like this:

"You see it now; I'm not afraid of it. It's very docile."

But the pocket watch acquired its true celebrity on parade, a few days before we embarked for Morocco. Sergeant Arango hastily formed us up, because he always showed up late. In the silence of the file, Villabona's watch panted like a vixen in a trap. First, the lieutenant inspected us; myopic, distracted, he stopped two or three times, inquiring about that unusual sound. Followed by the captain, tall and bent. He listened, without saying anything, and for a few minutes, seemed anxious while looking sideways around the file, until the lieutenant-colonel and the major arrived loudly arguing. Suddenly:

"Company! The colonel!"

The colonel was a corpulent, bad-tempered, old guy. He began putting a soldier in the second file, on a charge.

"This man doesn't have a mustache" he said, pointing out Pérez, a hairless youth who was studying mathematics.

"Well, actually, you see Your Honor, Sir …" answered the captain.

"I don't want excuses. I've said that everyone is to be shaved, and have a mustache. I don't want any ladies in my regiment. Mustache! Mustache!"

That outrageous call to whiskers produced a visible uneasiness in the other officers. They all looked on poor Pérez like a recidivist, an outlaw, a bad Spanish soldier. Pérez was shaking.

"Well, actually" the captain dared to venture, "this soldier can't grow a beard."

"Well, to the stockade, until he does."

After that verbal explosion, the silence was deep and anguished. Villabona's pocket watch could be heard even more clearly and precisely than ever. A spine-chilling fear ran through the ranks. The lieutenant-colonel looked at the major, and the captain looked at the lieutenant.

"What's this? Are there rats about?" said the colonel, casting his eye across the parade ground.

"Colonel, sir …" stuttered the captain.

—¡Ratas! ¡Ratas en la compañía! Esto es intolerable.

Fue cuando Carlitos Cabal, el pelotillero de la compañía, dijo con su voz quebrada:

—Es el reloj de Villabona.

—¿Un reloj? —gritó el coronel—. A ver, a ver.

Villabona, tembloroso, se desabrochó el correaje y sacó de su pantalón la causa de tanta inquietud.

La sorpresa de los jefes ante el monstruoso aparato era inenarrable.

—¡Qué barbaridad! —exclamó el coronel—. ¿Esto es un reloj? Capitán, ¿cómo consiente usted que un soldado vaya cargado con este artefacto?

Todos creíamos que después de aquella escena el capitán iba a enviar el reloj de Villabona al Parque de Artillería; pero no fue así. Villabona, ya en África, seguía transportando su reloj a lo largo de los convoyes y los parapetos.

Algún cabo bisoño reforzó las guardias del campamento ante el extraño ruido del reloj de Villabona. Éste, cuando no tenía servicio, permanecía en una esquina del barracón, como adormecido. Dijérase que el sonido del reloj era un idioma entrañable que sólo él entendía. Otro corazón oscuro, perdido en la campaña, ininteligible como el corazón de Villabona.

Estábamos en el Zoco-el-Arbaá de Beni Hassam y nos disponíamos a batir al Raisuni en Tazarut. Más de un año llevábamos en África. Por aquellos días empezó a decirse por la compañía que Villabona tenía un hijo.

—¿Es verdad eso, Villabona?

—Así dice la carta de mi padre.

—¿Pero no hace un año que no ves a tu mujer?

—Sí.

—¿Y entonces...?

Villabona se encogía de hombros.

—Cuando vuelvas a casa vas a encontrarte con dos o tres hijos más.

—Bueno.

Y hasta sonreía, como si le halagase aquella prole inesperada. Como si aquella feraz cosecha de hijos fuese dispuesta por el santo patrón de su parroquia.

Una mañana me tocó ir entre las fuerzas de protección de aguada. Iba también Villabona. Al hacer el despliegue, unos moros, parapetados detrás de una loma, nos tirotearon. Fue una agresión débil, aislada, de las muy frecuentes entonces en aquella guerra. Cuando el teniente nos reunió de nuevo, faltaba Villabona. Le encontramos detrás de una chumbera, llorando,

"Rats! Rats among the company! This is intolerable."
It was then that Carlitos Cabal, the company blue-eyed boy, timidly said:
"It's Villabona's pocket watch."
"A pocket watch?" bellowed the colonel. "Let's see, let's see."
Villabona, shaking, unbuckled his webbing and took that cause of such concern out of his pants.
The officers' surprise, when faced with that mechanism, was indescribable.
"How awful!" exclaimed the colonel. "Is this a pocket watch? Captain, how could you permit a soldier to be burdened with this object?"
After that scene, we all believed the captain would send Villabona's pocket watch to the Artillery Depot; but it did not happen. Once in Africa, Villabona went on carrying his pocket watch throughout convoy and guard duty.
Some green corporal reinforced the camp guard because of Villabona's noisy pocket watch. When he was not on duty, it stayed in a corner of the encampment, apparently sleeping. One might have said that the noise of the pocket watch was an unfathomable language that only he could understand. Another dark heart, lost in the campaign, unintelligible like Villabona's.
We were in Zoco-el-Arbaá de Beni Hassan preparing to do battle with El Raisuni[13] in Tazarut. We had been in Africa for more than a year. At that time, the rumor circulated in the company that Villabona had a son.
"Is that right, Villabona?"
"That's what my father's letter says."
"But isn't it a year since you've seen your wife?"
"Yes."
"And so …?"
Villabona shrugged his shoulders.
"When you go back home you're going to find yourself with two or three kids more."
"Good."
And he even smiled, as though flattered by unexpected offspring. It was as though that fertile harvest of children had been arranged by the patron saint of his parish.
One morning, it was my turn to be part of the escort for the water detail. Villabona was on it, too. On deploying, some Moors, under cover of a hill, began to fire on us. It was a weak, isolated, attack, very common then in that war. When the lieutenant regrouped us, there was no sign of Villabona. We found him behind a prickly-pear tree, crying, with his broken pocket watch

con el reloj deshecho entre las manos. Un proyectil enemigo se lo había destrozado. El reloj le había salvado la vida. Pero Villabona lloraba con un llanto dulce, desolado y persistente.

–Pero, hombre –le dijo el oficial–, ¿por qué lloras? Debieras estar muy contento. Vale más tu vida que tu reloj.

El soldado no oía. Sollozaba entre los escombros de su reloj, como si su vida no tuviera importancia al lado de aquel mecanismo que acababa de desintegrarse para siempre. De morir también.

in his hands. An enemy bullet had smashed it. The pocket watch had saved his life. But an anguished Villabona went on softly crying.

"But, man" said the officer, "why are you crying? You should be really happy. Your life is worth more than your pocket watch."

The soldier did not hear him. He was sobbing among the debris of his pocket watch, as though his life had no importance, compared to that mechanism which had just been smashed for ever. That had died.

3

CITA EN LA HUERTA

De mis tiempos de Marruecos, durante las difíciles campañas del 21, no logro destacar ningún episodio heroico. Por eso, cuando se habla de aquel pleito colonial y algún amigo mío relata con cierto énfasis la reconquista de Nador o el ataque a Magán, tomo una actitud prudente y no digo nada. Pero yo no tuve la culpa. Hasta creo que no carezco en absoluto de temperamento para dejarme matar con sencillez por cualquier idea abstracta. Los que me conocen saben que me batí una vez por el honor de una muchacha que luego resultó tanguista, y que en otra ocasión sostuve una polémica de prensa para reivindicar la figura histórica de Nerón, víctima de las gitanerías de Séneca. Yo no tuve la culpa de no ser héroe. Con mis leguis de algodón, mis guantes de gamuza, que originaban la furia de los sargentos por antirreglamentarios, y mi fusil R. 38.751, yo estaba dispuesto a tomar sitio en la Historia, así, sin darle importancia. Vivía esa época de la existencia en la cual nos seducen las más inútiles gallardías. Mi inclinación al heroísmo en aquella época no era sentimiento militar, facilitado en el cuartel al mismo tiempo que las municiones y el macuto; era una oleada de juventud, de altivez e indiferencia ante las cosas peligrosas de la vida. Aun siendo yo un recluta ilustrado, un *cuota*, con mi carrera casi terminada, no sentía ningún interés por el que llamaban «nuestro problema de África». Tampoco lograban conmoverme las palabras de los oficiales ni las órdenes y arengas que nos dirigían los jefes de los cuerpos expedicionarios. En cambio, me irritaban los relatos de los paqueos y las trágicas sorpresas en aguadas y convoyes.

En este estado de ánimo iba yo para héroe. Sin embargo, los dioses no me lo permitieron. En primer lugar, mi batallón fue destinado a Tetuán, en cuya zona la campaña era menos dura. Y cuando cierta mañana nos disponíamos a marchar al campo para cubrir posiciones de Beni Hassam, me llamó el capitán de mi compañía y me preguntó si sabía francés. Y como sabía francés, quedé destinado en la Alta Comisaría, donde, dicho sea de paso, jamás necesité el francés para nada. Allí se frustró mi vocación heroica.

3

TRYST IN THE ORCHARD

There were no heroic episodes of note in my time in Morocco during the difficult campaigns of '21. So, when they talk about that colonial quarrel, and some friend of mine, with a certain emphasis, relates the recapture of Nador or the attack on Magán, I adopt a prudent attitude and say nothing.[14] But it was not my fault. I actually believe that I definitely do not possess the temperament which would allow me to kill simply for some abstract idea. Those who know me are aware that I once fought for the honor of a girl who later turned out to be a cabaret hostess, and that on another occasion, I kept up a literary argument in the press in support of the historical figure of Nero, the victim of Seneca's trickery.[15] It was not my fault that I failed to become a hero. My cotton leggings and my chamois leather gloves had infuriated the sergeants for being non-regulation, yet armed with my R.38. 752 rifle, I was ready, without further ado, to take my place in History.[16] It was that time in life when we are seduced by pointless gallantries. My inclination to heroism in that period was not based on martial feelings issued in the store room along with ammunition and the knapsack; it was a wave of youthfulness, of arrogance and indifference towards life's dangers. Even though I was a college-educated recruit, a 'quota', with my studies almost completed, I did not feel the slightest interest in what was called 'our African problem.' Neither did the officers' words nor the orders, and the haranguing, meted out to us by the commanders of the Expeditionary Corps, have any effect; in fact, the tales of Moorish sniping and the tragic surprise ambushes at water holes and on convoys exasperated me.

In this state of mind I was set to be a hero. However, the gods put a stop to that. In the first place, my battalion was to be deployed to Tetouan, a zone where the campaign was less arduous. On one of those mornings when we were ready to march out to cover positions in Beni Hassan, the captain of my company called me out and asked me if I could speak French. As I could speak French, I was to be posted to the High Commission, where, as it happened, I never needed French for anything. My heroic calling was frustrated there and then.

De igual manera que carecía de sentido político no poseía la menor capacidad estética. La belleza de Tetuán no me impresionaba. Me parecía un pueblo sucio, maloliente, tenebroso aun en los días de sol. Al sol debía de sucederle lo que a mí, puesto que se vertía alborotadamente en todos aquellos lugares que, según los artistas, carecían de interés y de sugestión: la plaza de España, la calle de la Luneta, la carretera de Ceuta. Yo veía al sol muy europeizado y me sentía tan europeo como él.

En cambio, el barrio moro, los soportales de la alcazaba, las callejas que iban como sabandijas bajo arcos y túneles hasta sumirse en la boca húmeda de un portal, me aburrían inexorablemente. El sol tampoco llegaba hasta allí, y si llegaba era para tenderse, como un dogo, a los pies de una mora que permanecía en cuclillas sobre una terraza. Carlos Paredes, otro soldado que además era pintor, me reñía:

—Eres un bárbaro, chico, un bárbaro. Pero ¿qué te gusta a ti, vamos a ver?

—No sé, no sé. A veces pienso si me faltará espíritu; pero de repente me noto lleno de una ternura inesperada. Ya ves: a mí esas nubes sobre esa azotea, en este silencio de la tarde, me tienen sin cuidado. Pero de pronto pasa un soldado en alpargatas, con su lío al brazo, caminando penosamente hacia el campamento, y me emociona lo mismo que un hombre que va de camino, no sé por qué ni adónde, mientras nuestro automóvil traga carretera como un prestidigitador metros de cinta.

—¡Pero, hombre! ¡Tan bonito, abigarrado y curioso como es todo! Los tejedores de seda, los babucheros, los notarios, los comerciantes... Éste es un pueblo elegante y exquisito; está pulimentado por el tiempo, que es el que da nobleza y tono a la vida. En cambio, nuestra civilización todo lo hace ficticio y huidero; estamos enfermos de mentiras y de velocidad.

Las mujeres moras sí llegaron a obsesionarme. Ya he dicho antes que mi actitud de entonces ante las cosas era una mezcla de desprecio y desafío. Sólo una librera de la calle de la Luneta y algunas francesas de Tánger quedaron alucinadas en mi zona de seducción como dos avispas bajo un foco. Las hebreas bajaban los ojos con cierta frialdad de raza; me parecía estar mirando una ventana cuyos visillos corre de pronto una mano inadvertida. Las moras, no. Las moras reciben con desdén la mirada del europeo y la sepultan en sí mismas como los pararrayos hunden en tierra la electricidad. Quien las mira pierde toda esperanza de acercarse a ellas; van seguras y altivas por entre los hombres de otra raza, como los israelitas sobre las aguas dictadas por Dios. En vano perdí días enteros siguiendo finas

In the same way that I lacked political awareness, I possessed not the least aesthetic understanding. The beauty of Tetouan did not impress me. It seemed like a dirty, smelly, gloomy town, even on sunny days. The sun must have felt just like me, it poured light wildly in all those places which, according to artists, lacked interest and suggestiveness: the Plaza de España, Luneta Street, the Ceuta road. I saw it as a very European sun and I felt just as European.[17]

Whereas the Moorish quarter, the colonnades of the Alcazaba,[18] the little streets that moved like reptiles under the arches and tunnels to appear in the moist mouth of a doorway, bored me inexorably. The sun rarely got as far as that, and if it did, it would lie down, like a bull-mastiff at the feet of a Moorish girl sitting outside on her haunches. Carlos Paredes, another soldier who was also an artist, would remonstrate with me:

"Boy, you're awful, awful. But what do you like, let's see?"

"I don't know, I don't know. At times I do think I lack spirit, but then suddenly I'm filled with an unexpected tenderness. You see, those clouds above that roof, in this evening's silence, they don't have any effect on me. But suddenly if an espadrille-shod soldier walks by, with his bundle over his shoulder, painfully trudging towards the encampment, I become emotional just like a man going along a road, to I don't know where nor why, while our automobile eats up the highway like a conjurer eating up his meters of ribbon."[19]

"But, man! It's all so strange; it's so pretty and colorful! The silk weavers, the sandal vendors, the scribes, the merchants … This is an elegant and exquisite town; it's polished by time, that's what brings nobility and luminosity to life. Whereas our civilization makes everything fictitious and elusive; we're sick with lies and speed."

I became obsessed with Moorish women. I have said previously that my attitude to these things then, was a mixture of contempt and challenge. Only two females, a book seller in Luneta Street, and a Frenchwoman in Tangier, stayed beguilingly in my zone of seduction, like two wasps under a spotlight. The Jewish women lowered their eyes with a certain coldness of their race; I felt as though I were looking at a window where an unseen hand closes its lace drapes. It was not so with Moorish women. The Moorish women disdainfully meet the stares of Europeans and bury them within, in the way lightning conductors channel electricity through into the ground. Whoever looks at them loses all hope of knowing them; they walk by men of another race, self-assured and haughty, like the Israelites on the waters under God's sway. I lost whole days in vain, following fine, white silhouettes, which

siluetas blancas, que se me evaporaban en los portales como si no fuesen más que sutil tela de atmósfera.

El obstinado misterio de aquellas mujeres llegó a desvelarme a lo largo de los meses. Me volví malhumorado y colérico. Dos o tres veces engañé mi afán con mujeres del zoco que ejercían su oficio como las europeas; pero, al fin, mi deseo se veía burlado, como un cazador después de la descarga estéril. Yo quería desgarrar el secreto de una mujer mora, abrir un hueco en las paredes de su alma e instalar en ella mi amor civilizado y egoísta.

En otras palabras le dije un día esto mismo a Mohamed Haddú, hijo del Gran Visir, que era amigo mío del café. Haddú me repugnaba, porque era un señorito cínico, que se reía del Corán y de su raza; bebía mucho y se gastaba la plata hasaní del Gran Visir con las cupletistas españolas. Por entonces, Haddú perseguía a Gloria Cancio, tiple de una compañía de zarzuela que actuaba en el teatro Reina Victoria. Esta mujer era amiga mía de Madrid y cenaba conmigo algunas veces. Me fastidiaban su lagotería andaluza, sus mimos de gata sobona; a veces sentía deseos de quitarme de encima sus palabras como uno se quita los pelos del traje. A Haddú le gustaba Gloria. Ésta, en cambio, con notorio exceso de nacionalismo erótico y una más notoria falta de sentido práctico, me guardaba una fidelidad desagradable; odiaba al moro profundamente. Solía decirme:

—Cuando me mira, sus ojos me parecen los dos cañones de una pistola que me apunta.

—Pero está descargada, tonta.

Al conocer Haddú mi desventurado frenesí por las mujeres de su raza, me dijo:

—De modo que tú quieres casarte con una mora.

—¡Hombre! Tanto como casarme…

—Entonces, ¿qué quieres?

—Verla sin velos, tenerla cerca, que no me huya. Ser su novio, vaya.

—¡Oh, eso es muy difícil! —replicó Haddú—. Pero, oye —dijo después de meditar un poco—, podemos hacer una cosa: yo te llevo al lado de una mujer mora y tú me dejas el sitio libre con la cómica del Reina Victoria.

—Pero tiene que ser una mora de verdad, ¿eh? Una hija de familia, como dicen en España.

evaporated before me in the doorways as though they were nothing more than the subtle fabric of atmosphere.

The obstinate mystery of those women gave me sleepless nights throughout those months. I became bad-tempered and angry. Two or three times I cheated my obsession with women from the souk who plied their trade like European women; but, in the end, my desire was made a fool, like a hunter after a wasted shot. I wanted to unmask the secret of a Moorish woman, open a hole in the walls of her soul and install in her my civilized and egotistical love.

One day, in different words, I said the same thing to Mohamed Haddú, son of the Grand Vizier, who was a coffee shop friend of mine. Haddú disgusted me, because he was a cynical, young gentleman who laughed at the Koran and his race; he drank a lot and spent the Grand Vizier's Hassaní money[20] on Spanish cabaret singers. At that juncture, Haddú was chasing Gloria Cancio, a singer with a vaudeville troupe appearing at the Queen Victoria Theater. This woman was a friend of mine from Madrid and had dined with me on a few occasions. Her Andalusian flattery and her kitten cuddles annoyed me; at times, I felt like ridding myself of her words as one brushes hairs off clothing. Haddú liked Gloria. She, on the other hand, with a notorious excess of erotic patriotism and even more notorious lack of common sense, maintained a disagreeable fidelity to me; she profoundly disliked the Moor. She used to say to me:

"When he looks at me, his eyes are like a double-barreled pistol pointing at me."

"But it's not loaded, silly."[21]

When Haddú learned of my wretched obsession for women of his race, he said to me:

"So, you want to marry a Moorish girl."

"Man! I'm not saying I want to get married …"

"Then, what do you want?"

"I want to see her without her veil, to have her close to me, without her running off. Well, to be her boyfriend."

"Oh, that's very difficult!" replied Haddú. "But, listen," he said, after thinking about it for a little while, "we could do something: I'll take you up close to a Moorish woman and you leave me a free hand with the showgirl from the Queen Victoria."

"But it has to be a true Moorish girl, eh? A girl from a good family, as they say in Spain."

–Sí, hombre; mi hermana Aixa.

Aquel Haddú era un canallita. Quedamos en que yo citaría a Gloria para comer y en mi lugar iría el hijo del Gran Visir. Tampoco mi conducta con la tiple era ejemplar, ni mucho menos; pero no estaba yo entonces para sutilezas morales. Ante la probabilidad de conocer a una de aquellas mujeres imposibles y mezclar un poco de mi vida a la suya, estaba mi alma indomada, ambiciosa y dispuesta como una flecha en el arco.

Era una tarde llena de sol. Haddú y yo bajamos a la carretera de Ceuta por la pista del campamento. La casa del Gran Visir tenía a su espalda una de aquellas huertas jugosas y enormes que perfuman todo Yebala. A esta huerta habría de entrar yo para verme con Aixa. Los picachos de Gorgues cortaban por un lado el horizonte; más próximos, dulcificaban el paisaje los valles y cañadas cuya cintura ceñía el río. Recuerdo que topamos con uno de esos convoyes exiguos de los blocaos, un acemilero, un mulo, tres soldados y un cabo, que caminaban con aire de fatiga hacia los olvidados puestos de la montaña.

Hasta entonces no se me había ocurrido pensar en detalle la aventura. De pronto, me di cuenta de que iba a cometer una irreparable insensatez. ¿Qué papel sería el mío en la primera entrevista con una mujer exótica, cuyo idioma no conocía siquiera, separada de mí por el océano de una civilización? Pero ya era tarde para rectificar. Haddú abría en el mismo instante una puertecita colocada como un remiendo en la muralla de la huerta, y me empujaba nerviosamente. Me encontré de pronto, solo, bajo la mano de una palmera levantada en ceremoniosos adioses y al lado de una fuente cuyo vaporoso árbol de agua competía en claridad con los floridos naranjos próximos.

Y en simultáneo advenimiento apareció Aixa, indecisa y trémula, filtrándose como un poco de luz por el verde tabique de los rosales. Si Aixa fuera una muchacha europea me recordaría como un tonto; tan acobardado, inexpresivo e inmóvil me figuro a mí mismo en aquel momento. Tuve la gran suerte de que Aixa no fuese una señorita de la buena sociedad, acostumbrada a medir la timidez de sus pretendientes, sino una morita de apenas quince años que estaba delante de mí despidiendo sonrisas como una joya despide luz. Estaba sin velos y era como una chuchería recién comprada a la que acababan de quitar la envoltura de papel de seda. Morena. Pero una morenez de melocotón no muy maduro, con esa pelusa que hace la piel de la fruta tan parecida a piel de mujer.

La recordaré siempre delante de mí, porque mi estupor de entonces fue

"Yes, of course; my sister Aisha."

That Haddú was a swine. We agreed that I would arrange a dinner date with Gloria, and the son of the Grand Vizier would go in my place. My conduct with the cabaret singer was also far less than exemplary; but at that time, I was not concerned with moral subtleties. The probability of getting to know one of those impossible women and meld a little of my life with hers, had made my soul ambitiously indomitable and ready like an arrow on a bow.

It was a sunny afternoon. Haddú and I went down to the Ceuta road by the encampment track. The Grand Vizier's house backed onto one of those enormous, fructiferous orchards that perfume the whole of the Yebala region.[22] I would have to enter this orchard in order to see Aisha. On one side, the peaks of Gorgues[23] were silhouetted against the horizon, while closer, the landscape was softened by the valleys and ravines which fringed the river. I recall that we bumped into one of those exiguous blockhouse convoys, a muleteer, a mule, three soldiers and a corporal, walking with an exhausted air towards a forgotten position in the mountains.

Until that time, I had not given any thought to the details of that meeting. Suddenly, it hit me that I was about to commit an irreparable blunder. What would be my role in this first rendezvous with an exotic woman, whose language I did not even know, separated from me by the ocean of a civilization? But it was already too late to change my mind. At that very moment, Haddú was opening a small gate arranged like a patch in the orchard wall, and he nervously pushed me in. I suddenly found myself alone, under the raised hand of a palm tree as it ceremoniously waved its goodbyes and next to a fountain, whose vaporous, tree-shaped waters competed in clarity with the nearby flowering orange trees.

Aisha simultaneously appeared, unsure and trembling, insinuating herself like a tiny ray of sunlight through the green partition of rose bushes. Had Aisha been a European girl, I can imagine how stupid I would have looked, so cowed, inexpressive and motionless was I at that moment. I was truly fortunate that Aisha was not a young lady of good society used to measuring the timidity of her suitors, but rather a Moorish girl of hardly fifteen years of age, standing in front of me radiating smiles like a jewel scattering light. She was without a veil, and was like a recently bought trinket with its silk wrapping freshly removed. Dark-skinned. But of a darkness akin to an unripe peach, with that down which makes the fruit so like a woman's skin.

I will always recall her standing before me, because at that time, my

una especie de tinta china para estampar bien la imagen de Aixa en mi memoria. No llevaba velos. Un justillo de colores vivos, bordado en plata y oro, le cerraba el busto. Vestía también unos calzones anchos, como los holandeses, y se ceñía la cintura con una faja de seda azul. Llevaba medias blancas y babuchas rosadas guarnecidas de plata. La llamé al recobrarme:

−¡Aixa!

Se llevó el dedo índice a los labios recién pintados, se acercó a mí, lentamente, colocó sus manos de uñas rojas sobre mis hombros y estuvo contemplándome atentamente unos segundos. Y cuando yo quise prenderla con mis brazos tontos, mis brazos que aquel día no me sirvieron para nada, ella dio un brinco y se puso fuera de mi alcance. De un macizo de claveles, grande como un charco de sangre, arrancó uno, rojo, ancho y denso, y me lo arrojó como un niño arroja una golosina a un león enjaulado. Después huyó ligera y no la volví a ver. No sé cuánto tiempo estuve allí, al lado de la alta palma, extático, con el clavel en la mano como una herida palpitante.

En vano vigilé muchas tardes la huerta de Aixa y los ajimeces de su casa. En vano hablé a Haddú. No la volví a ver más.

Aquel suceso me desesperó tanto que pedí la incorporación a mi Cuerpo, destacado en Beni Arós. Nuestro campamento era como un nido sobre un picacho. Me pasaba los días durmiendo y paseando por el recinto, y las noches de servicio en el parapeto. Un día se destacó una sección de mi compañía para asistir a la boda de un caíd. Me tocó ir. El espectáculo era animado y pintoresco. Asistían los montañeses armados, las jarkas, los regulares. La caballería mora era como un mar ondulante, donde cada caballo resultaba una ola inquieta. El aire estaba repleto de gritos y de pólvora. Las barbas blancas de los caídes formaban un zócalo lleno de gracia y de majestad sobre la masa oscura de los moros jóvenes alineados al fondo.

Entre el estruendo y la algarabía de la fiesta vi aparecer a los nuevos esposos, a caballo. Los velos, las ajorcas y los collares de la mora refulgían espléndidamente. Miré sus ojos. ¡Oh, Aixa! La novia era Aixa, la hija del Gran Visir. Aquellos ojos eran los mismos que me alucinaron una tarde en Tetuán y que yo llevaba como dos alhajas en el estuche de mi memoria. Ella no me vio. ¡Cómo me iba a ver! En la larga fila vestida de caqui, yo era el número dieciocho para doblar de cuatro en fondo.

No recuerdo bien lo que sucedió después. Pero debí de cometer muchas inconveniencias, porque cuando regresamos al destacamento oí que el teniente decía al capitán, señalándome:

stupor became a species of Indian ink stamping Aisha's image firmly in my memory. She was not wearing a veil. A jerkin of bright colors, edged in gold and silver, enclosed her bosom. She was wearing wide pants, too, like the Dutch, and she secured them at the waist with a blue, silk cummerbund. She had white stockings and pink sandals set with silver. When I recovered myself, I called out:

"Aisha!"

She put her index finger to her recently painted lips. Then she came close to me, slowly, placed her red-nailed hands on my shoulders and looked at me attentively for a few seconds. And when I wanted to hold her in my crazed arms, arms which that day, were of no use to me, she skipped away out of my reach. From a clump of carnations, large like a pool of blood, she picked one, red, wide and thick, and threw it towards me like a child throwing a titbit to a caged lion. Then she daintily fled and I did not see her again. I do not know how long I was there, next to the high palm tree, ecstatic, with the carnation in my hand like a palpitating wound.

In vain, I spent many afternoons watching Aisha's orchard and the lattice windows of her house. In vain I spoke to Haddú. I never saw her again.

That incident drove me so wild that I requested to be returned to my Corps, deployed in Beni Arós. Our encampment was like a nest on top of a peak. I spent the days sleeping and walking about the compound, and the nights on guard. One day a platoon from my company was detached to attend the wedding of a *kaid*,[24] and I went with it. It was a lively and picturesque spectacle. There were armed hill-men, *harkas*[25] and *Regulares*.[26] The Moorish cavalry was like a moving sea, in which every horse created a restless wave. The air was full of cries and gunpowder. The *kaids'* white beards formed a graceful and majestic backdrop above the dark mass of young Moors stretching out below.

In among the din and the hullabaloo of the feast I saw the newlyweds appear, on horseback. The veils, bracelets and necklaces of the Moorish woman shone splendidly. I looked her in the eye. Oh Aisha! The bride was Aisha, the daughter of the Grand Vizier. Those eyes were the same ones that had fascinated me one evening in Tetouan, and which I kept in the treasure box of my memory like two jewels. She did not see me. How could she have seen me! In the large khaki-clad squad, I was number eighteen in the four deep file.

I do not really recall what happened next. But I must have made a mess of things, because when we returned to the detachment, I overheard the lieutenant say to the captain, pointing to me:

–Este chico no parece estar en sus cabales. Sería conveniente que fuese al hospital para que lo vieran.

Nada de esto tiene, sin duda, importancia; pero es lo único saliente que me ha sucedido en Marruecos. Lo cuento porque dejó en mí un desasosiego especial, algo como la sensación ínfima, penosa y lejana de una herida ya en cicatriz.

"This boy doesn't seem to be in his right mind. He should be looked at in the hospital."

Doubtless, none of this is important; but it is the only noteworthy thing that has happened to me in Morocco. I relate it because it left me with a particular anxiety, something like the dreadful, painful and distant feeling of a wound, already a scar.

4

MAGDALENA ROJA

Confieso que la única persona que me desconcertaba en las juntas del Sindicato era la compañera Angustias. Ya entonces tenía yo fama de orador. Cuando pedía la palabra en el tumulto de las discusiones, se apaciguaba el oleaje verbal, y los camaradas, aun aquellos que a lo largo del discurso habían de interrumpirme con frases más duras, adoptaban una postura cómoda para escucharme.

–Callarse. A ver qué dice el *Gafitas*.

Debía el apodo a mi presbicia precoz, disimulada por las gafas de concha. En realidad, la mitad de mis éxitos oratorios nacen de este defecto óptico. Ya en pie, los oyentes, uno a uno, no existían para mí. Tenía delante una masa espesa, indeterminada, convertida, todo lo más, en materia dialéctica. Como no veía concretamente a nadie, ni llegaban a mí los gestos de aprobación o desagrado, exponía fácilmente mis ideas y permanecía aislado de toda coacción externa. Eso me daba un aplomo y una serenidad de tal índole que mis palabras se ceñían al argumento como la piel al hueso. A veces, una opinión mía provocaba una tempestad de gritos. Pero mi voz se abría paso como el rayo entre el clamor de la tormenta. A veces me insultaban:

–¡Charlatán! ¡Político!

–¡Palabras, no! ¡Acción!

–¡Intelectual! Sois una m… los intelectuales.

–¡Niño! ¿Qué sabes tú de eso?

Esta interrupción era la que prefería Angustias y me azoraba mucho. Porque yo comprendía que a mis discursos les faltaba la autoridad que dan los años. Era demasiado joven para conducir aquella milicia frenética de alpargatas, de trajes de mahón, con el alma curtida por el rencor de muchos siglos de capitalismo. Para ellos las palabras mágicas eran «huelga», «sabotaje», «acción directa». Yo sabía lanzarlas a tiempo, seguro de su efecto. Pero, enseguida, la asamblea se daba cuenta de que aquel que las pronunciaba las había aprendido en Marx o en Sorel y no en la bárbara escuela del trabajo manual. Aun ahora echo de menos en mi espíritu la disciplina del proletario, del hombre que ha conocido la esclavitud de la ignorancia y del jornal. Sólo ése posee un corazón implacable, ciego y cruel, un corazón revolucionario.

4

RED MAGDALENE

I admit that the only person who flustered me in Union meetings was comrade Angustias.[27] By that time, I had gained a reputation as an orator. When I requested the floor amid the maelstrom of meetings, the verbal swell would calm, and the comrades, even those who constantly heckled me, would sit back in order to hear me out.

"Pipe down. Let's see what *Specks* has to say."

I owed the nickname to my extreme short-sightedness, covered up by my tortoiseshell spectacles. In reality, half of my oratory success stems from this optical defect. By the time I stood up, the listeners, as individuals did not exist for me. I had before me a thick, indeterminate mass, all the rest turned into dialectical material. As I could not see anyone clearly, and as their gestures of approbation or displeasure did not strike home, I was able to expound my ideas easily and remain isolated from all external pressure. This gave me an assurance and calmness, making my words cling to the argument like skin to the bone. Sometimes an opinion of mine would provoke a tempest of shouting. But my voice cleared the way like a bolt of lightning through the din of the storm. At times, they would insult me:

"Charlatan! Politician!"

"Not words! Actions!"

"Intellectual! You intellectuals are a bunch of s—…"

"Hey rich kid! What do you know about all this?"

This was Angustias' preferred interruption and it bothered me a lot. Because I knew that my speeches lacked the authority that comes with age. I was too young to control that frenetic militia of espadrilles, of denim overalls; souls seared by the bitterness of many centuries of capitalism. For them, the magic words were 'strike', 'sabotage', 'direct action.' I knew when to use them, sure of their effect. But the meeting quickly realized that the person who uttered those words had learned them from Marx or in Sorel[28] and not in the brutal school of manual work. Even now I lack that proletarian, disciplined spirit, of the man who has known the slavery of ignorance and casual work. He alone possesses an implacable, blind and cruel heart, a revolutionary heart.

Yo, ¿por qué negarlo?, era un muchacho de la clase media, un *dilettante* del obrerismo. El «gran hecho ruso», como llamaban los semanarios a la dictadura de Lenin, me había entusiasmado de tal modo que me di de alta en el Sindicato Metalúrgico. Yo era perito químico en una fábrica de metales y estaba a punto de obtener el título de ingeniero. En mi cuarto había una cabeza de Lenin dibujada por mí mismo; una gran cabeza mongólica, a la que contemplaba con exaltada ternura, mientras abajo, en la calle, corrían, alegres, los automóviles charolados. Muchas veces evoco aquel cuarto, donde mis pasos latían como un rumor de la propia entraña del mundo. ¡Qué impaciencia por vivir, por luchar, por dejar de ser una oscura gota del torrente urbano! Y, a veces, el generoso pesimismo de los veinte años, el vago anhelo de morir por el simple hecho de que una mujer no se ha fijado en nosotros, o porque estuvimos torpes en una disputa, o porque el correo no ha traído la cita ofrecida la noche antes. En aquel cuarto esculpía mi pensamiento universos que minutos después quedaban convertidos en polvo.

Pero, siempre, mi conciencia acechaba como un centinela que tuviese la consigna de la duda. Yo me encontraba sin fuerzas para trazar una vida dura, obstinada, rectilínea. Lenin, huraño, enfermo, mal alimentado en su cuchitril de Berna, sin ropa para salir a la calle, era el atroz remordimiento de mi soledad. Porque yo sentía la carne gravitar constantemente sobre mi espíritu, y toda la vida circundante se convertía en tentación de mis sentidos. No era puro mi rencor contra el burgués del automóvil y del abrigo de pieles. Y, sin embargo, no podía ser más repugnante aquella multitud ventruda y cerril que llenaba los teatros y los salones de té y se esparcía por toda la ciudad con su escandaloso rastacuerismo.

Pero el rival más temible de mi obra era el deseo erótico. Yo iba por las calles enredándome en todas las miradas de mujer; y tenía que ir quitándolas de mis pasos como si fueran zarzas o espinos. Aquello me perdía para la *causa*. Pascual, el líder, con su sonrisa, que era lo mismo que una grieta de sol entre la nube de la barba, me disculpaba con frecuencia:

–Este *Gafitas* es un muchacho que quiere sorberse el mundo con una paja, como quien se toma un refresco. Ya parará.

Angustias, sin embargo, no me lo perdonaba. Tan altiva, tan firme, tan fanática. Según ella, yo no tenía más que una visión literaria de la vida y en la primera ocasión me pasaría al campo de enfrente.

–Usted –solía decirme– no es de los nuestros. Usted es un señorito. No, no se enfade, *Gafitas*; usted no tiene la culpa. El atavismo, hijo, el atavismo. Mi

And, why deny it? I was a middle class boy, a *dilettante* worker. The "great
Russian event," as the weeklies called Lenin's dictatorship, had inspired me
to such an extent that I joined the Metalworkers' Union.[29] I was a chemistry
technician in a metals factory and I was on the point of obtaining a degree
in engineering. In my room was my own drawing of Lenin's head; a large
Mongolian head, which I looked at with extreme fondness, while below,
in the street, cheerful, shiny automobiles sped about. Many are the times I
recall that room, where my footsteps beat like the murmur of the very entrails
of the world. What impatience to live, to strive, to cease being an obscure
drop in the urban torrent! And, at times, in the generous pessimism of my
twenty years, the vague longing for death, simply because a woman had
taken no notice of me, or because I had appeared awkward in an argument,
or because the mail had not brought me the offered date of the night before.
In that room I sculpted universes in my mind, which moments later, were
turned to dust.

But my conscience, like a sentry's duty of doubt, always lay in wait
for me. I found myself lacking the strength to devise a hard, obstinate or
rectilinear life. Lenin, unsociable, sick, ill-nourished in his hovel in Bern,
lacking clothes to go out in, was my solitude's cruel remorse. Because I
felt the flesh constantly bearing down on my spirit, and all life around me
became the temptation of my senses. My bitterness against the bourgeoisie
in automobiles and fur coats was not genuine. And yet, that pot-bellied and
uncouth multitude which filled the theaters and the tea-rooms and spread
its scandalous ostentation throughout the city could not have been more
repugnant.

But the most feared rival of my work was erotic desire. I would walk
down the street caught up in every woman's glance; I had to brush them
away as though they were brambles or thorns. That lost me to the 'cause'.
Pascual, the leader, with a smile like a chink of sun between clouds of beard,
frequently forgave me:

"*Specks* here, is a kid who wants to suck the whole world up through a
straw, like someone having a drink. He'll get over it."

Angustias, however, did not forgive me. She was so determined, so strong
and so fanatical. According to her, I held nothing more than a literary vision
of life and on the first opportunity I would change sides.

"You," she would say to me, "are not one of us. You're a young gentleman.
No, don't get angry *Specks*; it's not your fault. It's atavism, kid, atavism. My

odio contra todo esto ha venido acumulándose de generación en generación
y estallará en mí cuando esta mano, esta que usted ve tan pequeña, lance la
bomba en una iglesia, en un banco o en uno de esos reales clubes que hay
por ahí.

–Esa mano –le contestaba yo en voz baja– no tirará más que besos.

–¡Puaf! ¡Qué asco me da usted! Como los señoritos. Como los señoritos.

Los compañeros decían que Angustias era la amante de Pascual
Domínguez; pero no pude comprobarlo nunca. Es cierto que aquella mujer
áspera, dominante, voluntariosa, era otra al lado del viejo propagandista. Pero
más bien su actitud de entonces parecía de discípulo, de escolar que aprende
la más difícil asignatura. Cuando Pascual hablaba con su voz sustanciosa y
caliente, Angustias sufría algo así como una transfiguración. Resplandecían
sus ojos metálicos, y seguían, anhelantes, el ademán y la palabra, como
golondrinas detrás de la golondrina guía. Lo que más fácilmente se confunde
con el enamoramiento es la admiración.

Pascual Domínguez la había encontrado en América, durante uno de sus
viajes de agitador. Se decía que Angustias había sido corista de zarzuela,
maestra rural y querida de un millonario. Pero nadie conocía, a ciencia cierta,
su pasado. Cuando yo la conocí era ya una mujer de más de treinta años, con
el cuerpo duro y firme y el cabello negro y brillante como el plumaje de los
cuervos. Se ganaba la vida haciendo muñecas de trapo, de esas que se ven en
los grandes bazares, en los gabinetes de las casas elegantes y en las alcobas
de las meretrices de precio. Yo la irritaba con mis bromas.

–Anoche he visto una de sus muñecas en casa de una amiga mía. Es
preciosa.

–¿Quién? ¿La amiga?

–No, no. La muñeca.

Me lanzaba, como dos piedras, sus ojos iracundos; pero yo creo que era
para disimular algo. Porque Pascual me lo dijo una tarde:

–Es curioso lo que le sucede a Angustias. Ya la oye usted despotricar contra
los trabajadores que tienen hijos, porque dice que es criminal prolongar
el dolor del mundo. Afirma que es preciso destruirlo con la infecundidad.
Pues bien, quiere a sus muñecas como si fueran hijas suyas. Recorre los
escaparates para verlas por última vez. A veces llega con el semblante opaco
y me dice: «La del Bazar González, aquella del sombrerito verde, ya no
está». Y añade: «Bueno, era graciosilla, ¿verdad?».

A los pocos días, por mortificar a Angustias, escribí estas cuartillas y se
las mandé a su casa por un *continental*:

hatred against it all has been accumulating from generation to generation and it will burst out of me when this hand, this hand which looks so small to you, throws a bomb into a church, a bank or one of those royalist clubs hereabouts.'

"That hand" I answered "will throw nothing more than kisses."

"Ugh! You make me sick! You talk like a rich kid, just like a rich kid."

The comrades said that Angustias was Pascual Domínguez's lover; but I was never able to prove it. That sharp-tongued woman was certainly dominant and headstrong, but she was different when with the old propagandist. But her attitude back then was rather more of the disciple; like a schoolgirl learning the most difficult subject. When Pascual spoke in his weighty and passionate voice, Angustias experienced something akin to a transfiguration. Her metallic eyes would shine and longingly follow the gesture and word, like swallows behind the guiding bird. It is very easy to confuse love with admiration.

Pascual Domínguez had met her in America, during one of his tub-thumping tours. It is said that Angustias had been a chorus girl in vaudeville, a country school teacher and a millionaire's mistress. But no-one knew her past for sure. When I got to know her, she was a woman already turned thirty years of age, with a hard, firm body and black, shiny hair like a raven's plumage. She earned a living making ragdolls, the type that one sees in the large toy stores, in the studies of elegant homes and in the bedrooms of high class prostitutes. My jokes would make her angry.

"Last night I saw one of your ragdolls in a girlfriend's house. Really lovely."

"Who? The girl?"

"No, no. The ragdoll."

Her eyes pierced mine like two angry stones; but I think it was to hide something. Because Pascual said to me one day:

"It's strange what goes on with Angustias. You've already heard her speaking her mind against workers who have children, because she says that it's criminal to prolong the world's pain. She asserts that it's necessary to destroy it with infertility. But she loves her ragdolls as though they were her daughters. She goes around the store windows to see them one last time. Sometimes she comes to me with a gloomy face and says: 'The one in González Toy Store, the one with the little green hat, it's no longer there.' And she adds: "Well, it was really cute, wasn't it?"

A little while later, I wrote these lines just to tease Angustias, and sent them to her home through the *Continental* telegraph agency.

«Carta de mamá a la muñeca del sombrerito verde. En el hotel de Consuelo López, bailarina de el Cabaret Rojo.

Niña mía: Ayer fui a verte, por la mañana. La mañana era como una esfera de cristal, tan frágil que yo temía verla romperse con los bocinazos de los automóviles y los timbres de los tranvías. A las puertas de los cafés brotaba el arco iris de los aperitivos. Por las aceras, con libros debajo del brazo y alguna con un violín enfundado, iban niñas como tú, mayores que tú, con más vida que la que yo te di, muñequita perdida ya para mis manos. Los húsares, con sus grandes plumas; los barquilleros, con su caja a la espalda como otro barquillo rojo y tremendo; las *nurses*, vestidas de chocolate; todo lo que a ti te encantaría desde tu escaparate delirante de colores y destellos. Había también mujeres con pieles, y como llevaban abrigos abiertos, diríanse rajadas desde el cuello hasta los muslos para enseñar por la herida reciente los intestinos de crespón de los vestidos.

Yo iba a verte otra vez, hija de mis horas de obrera, a esa inclusa del bazar donde ya jamás podré recuperarte. Y al ver que no estabas, el odio que llevo encharcado en las entrañas afluía a mi boca y a mis ojos. Me daban ganas de insultar a los transeúntes, a esas mujeres elegantes y despreocupadas a quienes divierten mis muñecas. Porque nadie sabe el seco dolor que me has costado y la amargura que han bebido mis pinceles para crear el alegre mohín de tus labios y tus ojos. Ahora te veo reclinada en un diván frente a la porcelana japonesa y el indispensable mantón de flecos. El gabinete de una cupletista española está amueblado por el estilo de su alma, que tiene por todo adorno un cuplé patriótico, unos versos de revista ilustrada y una cartilla de la Caja de Ahorros. Te compadezco, niña mía, porque tú, tan pintoresca, tan moderna, tendrás que soportar el álbum de postales iluminadas, el piano que no sabe más música que la de Guerrero y el patán ensortijado que saliva en el piso y devora ronchas de jamón a las tres de la mañana.

Perdóname. Yo no quise darte un destino tan duro. Me consuela pensar que algún día se abrirá para ti la tumba de un baúl, o que perecerás en las manos de una niña que querrá descubrir el secreto de mi arte de hacer muñecas».

Al día siguiente encontré a Angustias en el Centro y me increpó:

–He quemado sus cuartillas, y enseguida me lavé los dedos, no tan manchados de ceniza como de sensiblería. ¡Pero qué literato más cursi es

"Letter from mom to the ragdoll with the little green hat. At the hotel of Consuelo López, dancer in the 'Red Cabaret'.

My child: yesterday morning I went to see you. The morning was like a crystal sphere, so fragile, that I was afraid the automobiles' horns and the trolley cars' bells might shatter it. In the café doorways, a rainbow of aperitifs arose. Little girls like you and older than you, with more life than I gave you, my lost little doll, went by on the sidewalks with books under their arms and one with a cased violin. Hussars, with their large plumes; waffle sellers with their traditional, round, tin boxes on their backs looking themselves like an enormous, red waffle box,[30] nurses, dressed in chocolate brown; everything that would captivate you from your deliriously colorful, glittering, store window. There were also women in furs, their coats slit open from neck to thigh displaying through that recent wound their dresses' crepe intestines.

I went to see you again, daughter of my working hours, even to the toy store where I could never retrieve you. And, when I saw that you were not there, the hatred I carry deep within my guts flowed into my mouth and my eyes. It made me want to curse the passers-by, those unconcerned, elegant women who are amused by my dolls. Because no-one understands the dull pain that you have cost me and the bitterness that my paint brushes have drunk in order to create the happy expression on your lips and in your eyes. I can see you now, reclining on a couch in front of a piece of Japanese porcelain and the indispensable fringed shawl. The sitting room of a Spanish cabaret singer is furnished to suit her soul, its only ornament, a patriotic vaudeville lyric, some lines from an illustrated magazine and a savings bank book. I feel sorry for you, my child, because, you who are so picturesque, so modern, will have to tolerate an album of colored postcards, the piano that knows only the music of Guerrero,[31] and the curly-haired lout who spits on the floor and devours ham sandwiches at three o'clock in the morning.

Forgive me. I did not want to give you such a bleak future. I console myself in the thought that one day they will open a trunk tomb for you, or that you will perish at the hands of a little girl wanting to discover the secret of my art of making ragdolls."

I met Angustias the following day at the Union Building and she rebuked me:

"I burned your notes, and immediately washed my fingers, not so much stained with ashes as with sentimentality. But what a literary snob you are!

usted! ¿Y usted quiere hacer la revolución? ¡Vamos, hombre! Dedíquese a escribir novelas blancas para las burguesitas. A mí me importan un rábano mis muñecas después de venderlas. Y antes también. Porque me da rabia pensar en el esfuerzo que me cuestan. Lo de menos es que diviertan a las señoritas estúpidas. Me irrita, sobre todo, tener que dedicarme a esto.

–Entonces, ¿qué querría usted hacer?

–¿Yo?

Iba a decírmelo, pero se arrepintió en el acto:

–Nada, nada, *Gafitas*. ¿Para qué vamos a hablar? No merece la pena.

Lo cierto es que Angustias, a fuerza de altivez, se apoderaba de los resortes de mi vida. Yo veía que mi vida estaba entre sus manos. Pero lo inquietante era sentirme entre sus manos como una cosa inútil, más inútil que el paño o el cartón de sus muñecas. Angustias valoraba a los hombres por su capacidad revolucionaria; era una obrera de la idea. Ante un obrerillo insignificante que acariciaba a escondites su *star*, como quien mima un tigre domesticado, le centelleaban los ojos igual que carbones removidos. Le decía:

–¿Qué tal? ¿La has probado?

–Sí. El otro día en los desmontes. Es superior.

–Pero las armas no valen nada. Hay que tener corazón.

–¡Anda! ¡Pues claro! Yo lo tengo. Que se atrevan los del Libre…

–Di que sí, chico. Para eso eres hombre. ¡Duro con los esquiroles!

Una tarde salía yo de casa y me encontré a Angustias en la calle. Era al anochecer y la ciudad acababa de prenderse los alfileres de sus focos para entrar, brillante y dadivosa, en una tibia noche de mayo. Serpenteaban los anuncios luminosos, como si estableciesen pugilato con los timbres y las bocinas de los coches. Las gentes se agrupaban en las taquillas de los cines, o formaban murallas humanas al borde de la acera, esperando que los guardias, con gesto de domadores, detuviesen el rebaño de bestias mecánicas.

–Adiós, Angustias.

–Sería raro no encontrarle; usted anda por la calle a todas horas. Detrás de alguna chica, ¿eh?

–Pues no. Salía a dar un paseo.

–Lo mismo que yo. Esta tarde estaba aburrida. Casi, casi, melancólica.

–¡Qué raro!

–Sí, es raro; esto no me da nunca. Lo que hago es ponerme de mal humor.

–¿Quiere usted que sigamos juntos?

Do you really want to start the revolution? Come on man! You get on with writing bland novels for little bourgeois girls. I don't give a damn about my dolls once they're sold. Or before, for that matter. It makes me angry to think about the effort I put into them. At least it may entertain stupid young ladies. Above all, it annoys me that I have to spend time doing it."[32]

"Then, what would you like to do?"

"Me?"

She was just about to tell me; but she thought better of it: "Nothing, nothing, *Specks* Why are we talking about it? It's not worth the effort."

What is certain is that Angustias, by dint of her arrogant attitude, was taking over my life. I saw that my life was in her hands. But it was disquieting to feel myself in her hands like a useless thing, more useless than the cloth or cardboard of her ragdolls. Angustias valued men for their revolutionary capacity; she was a worker of ideas. Faced with an insignificant little worker, who cuddled his *Star* pistol,[33] like someone caressing a domesticated tiger, her eyes blazed like stirred up coals. She said:

"So how was it? Did you try it?"

"Yes. The other day in a clearing. It's excellent."

"But weapons are a waste of time. You need guts."

"Come on! I know I have them! Just let the bosses' gunmen dare …"

"Well said, kid. Now you're a man. Hit the scabs hard!"

One evening, as I was leaving home, I bumped into Angustias in the street. It was dusk; the city's lamps were beginning to shed brilliant light into the balmy May night. The snaking neon-lit signs seemed about to tussle with the automobiles' bells and horns. People gathered in the box offices at the movie theaters, or formed human walls on the edge of the sidewalk, waiting for the doormen who with trainers' gestures, would halt the flock of mechanical beasts.

"Hello, Angustias."

"It would be funny not to bump into you; you're out in the street at all hours. After a girl, huh?"

"Well, no. I've come out for a walk."

"Me, too. I was bored this evening. Almost, almost melancholic."

"That's strange!"

"Yes, it's strange; this never happened before. It's put me in a bad mood."

"Shall we walk on together?"

–Bueno.

–Podemos entrar en un café de éstos a tomar cualquier cosa.

–No. En los del centro no me gusta. Vamos a un bar de barrio, de esos que tienen pianola.

Abandonamos las calles céntricas y atravesamos pasadizos angostos alumbrados con gas.

De vez en cuando teníamos que dejar la acera porque tropezábamos con parejas de novios adosadas a las fachadas y a las vallas. De las tabernas salían bocanadas de escándalo con alguna blasfemia silbando como una bala. Angustias censuraba siempre:

–Esto es lo que nos pierde. Son brutos; no piensan y se someten.

–No se empeñe usted, Angustias. La disciplina quitará interés a la vida. Reglamentarlo todo, someter la existencia a una organización, quizá nos haga más infelices.

Los ojos de Angustias fosforecían en la sombra:

–Pues mientras tanto no seremos la fuerza, no seremos nada.

–Pero ¿por qué está usted tan resentida con la vida? ¿Qué le ha pasado a usted?

No me contestó porque entrábamos en una animada calle de los suburbios.

–Aquel bar me gusta. A veces vengo aquí con Pascual.

Entramos. No había mesas vacías y el camarero nos colocó en la que ocupaban dos individuos con traza y gesto de chóferes. Discutían mucho acerca de una mujer.

–Te aseguro que es una birria en cuanto se quita la ropa.

–Me vas tú a decir… ¡Vamos, hombre!

Pedimos dos vermuts. Un endiablado *jazz band* negro alborotaba, incansable, entre la indiferencia de la clientela que hablaba a gritos para imponerse a la música y consumía aperitivos y aceitunas. Angustias, volcando sobre mí las sombras más ocultas de sus ojos, me dijo:

–En efecto, *Gafitas*; yo soy una resentida, como usted dice. ¿Usted sabe por qué yo no he querido entrar antes en uno de esos cafés del centro? Porque ahí está todo mi pasado. Sí, mi pasado, mi vileza. Yo he vestido pieles y he tenido automóvil a mi puerta. Esto parece un folletín, pero es una historia. Y un día, ¡me daba aquello tanto asco!, la ciudad, el hotel, el hombre de las joyas, todo, que lo tiré como quien tira un cesto de basura a un vertedero. De repente, aquí, en la entrañas, sentí que me nacía la conciencia; una cosa muy rara, un odio, un rencor… Ahora padezco más pensando en mi juventud que en mi hambre de niña. A nadie se lo cuento. ¿Para qué? Pero hoy me han

"Fine."

"We could have something to drink in one of these cafés."

"No. I don't like these downtown cafés. Let's go to a local bar, one of those with a pianola."

We left the main streets and crossed narrow, little, gas-lit alleyways. From time to time, we had to step off the sidewalk because we were walking into couples leaning against walls and billboards. Uproarious blasts and the odd curse whistled out of the bars like a bullet. Angustias was always critical:

"This is where we lose out. They're brutes; they don't think and they go along with things."

"Don't start, Angustias. Discipline takes interest out of life. Regimenting everything, submitting our existence to an organization would maybe make us unhappier."

Angustias' eyes were phosphorescent in the gloom.

"As long as we're without power, we'll have nothing."

"But why are you so resentful of life? What can have happened to you?"

She did not answer me because we turned onto a busy, suburban street.

"I like that bar. I sometimes come here with Pascual."

We went in. There were no vacant tables, so the waiter put us at a table with two men who looked and sounded like cab drivers. They were busy talking about a woman.

"I'm telling you, when she strips off, she's freakish."

"That's what you say … Come on man!"

We ordered two vermouths. The customers were downing their aperitifs and olives, and shouting to each other, to make themselves heard above the devilish din of the tireless, black jazz band. Angustias, pouring the hidden depths of her eyes onto me, said:

"Well, *Specks* as you say, I'm resentful. Do you know why I didn't want to go into one of those downtown cafés? Because that's where all my past is. Yes, my past, my depravity. I've worn fur coats and had an automobile at my door. This sounds like a melodrama, but it's my life. One day, I got so fed up with it, the city, the hotel, the guy with the jewelry, everything. I junked it like someone throwing a can of garbage into a dump! Suddenly, I had a feeling here in my gut that I was giving birth to my conscience; it was a strange thing, hatred, a grudge… I hurt more now, thinking about my youth than about my childhood hunger. I've never told anyone. What's the

dado tristeza la calle y la casa. Hasta ese *jazz band* que toca tan inútilmente.

—¡Magdalena roja!

Y en aquel mismo instante vi a aquella mujer tan alejada de mí, con un alma tan diferente a la mía, que la hubiera estrangulado en un abrazo.

A los pocos días se declaró una huelga general. Las patrullas de caballería resonaban dramáticamente en la oquedad de las calles sin vehículos. Cientos de obreros, como hormigas ociosas, entraban y salían en el Centro a inquirir noticias, a disputar y a comentar el conflicto que tenía suspensa y atemorizada a la ciudad. Los más extremistas, azuzados por Angustias, hablaban de utilizar las pistolas contra los guardias. Pascual Domínguez, sin embargo, no era partidario en aquella ocasión de la violencia, porque sabía que los sindicatos no estaban todavía preparados para una lucha así. Con el pretexto de unos despidos, él había iniciado la huelga a modo de un recuento de fuerzas. Todos sus discursos tendían a sujetar a aquella fiera policéfala, desmelenada, que vibraba en los bancos mugrientos cada vez que se hablaba de la tiranía patronal.

—Daremos la batalla —me decía Domínguez— cuando se nos crea atemorizados. Angustias se había aliado con los elementos comunistas y anarquistas y predicaba el terrorismo a espaldas de Pascual Domínguez. Una tarde me llamó.

—*Gafitas*, usted es un cobarde. Debí de palidecer de rabia.

—Y usted una imprudente, Angustias.

—Un cobarde. Porque Pascual aconseja calma lleno de responsabilidad. Pero usted lo hace porque le falta corazón.

—Me sobra para todo; hasta para meterla a usted en él para siempre.

—Lo que yo digo: un corazón de tanguista. Y si no, demuéstrelo usted.

—Tonterías no.

—¡Qué juventud tan reflexiva! Es usted un excelente hijo de familia.

—¡No me irrite!

—¡Cobarde! ¡Cobarde! ¿A que no se atreve a acompañarme esta tarde?

—¿Adónde? ¡Alguna locura!

—A la fábrica de hilados. Pondré una bomba.

—No haga usted eso.

—Lo haré.

—Lo echará a perder todo.

—Mejor. Necesito sangre, incendio. ¡Muerte!

point? But today, I'm saddened by the street, my home and this jazz band's pointless music."

"Red Magdalene!"

I saw in that moment, a woman who was so remote from me, with a soul so totally different to mine, yet I could have hugged her to death.

A few days later a general strike was declared. The mounted patrols dramatically echoed in the hollow streets, empty of vehicles. Hundreds of workers, like idle ants, went in and out of the Union Building to get news, argue and comment on the conflict which had frightened and bewildered the city. The real extremists, egged on by Angustias, talked of using their weapons against the police. However, Pascual Domínguez was not for violence on that occasion, because he knew that the Unions were still not prepared for such a struggle. On the pretext of some layoffs, he had called the strike as a means of mustering forces. All his speeches tended to keep in check that disheveled, many-headed beast of revolutionary violence, shaking on those grimy benches every time that he spoke of the bosses' tyranny.[34]

"We'll take them on," Domínguez said to me, "when they think we're scared."

Angustias had allied herself with the communist and anarchist elements preaching terrorism behind Pascual Domínguez's back. One day, she said to me...

"*Specks*, you're a coward."

I must have blanched with rage.

"And you're shameless Angustias."

"You're a coward. Because Pascual's advice is to stay calm and controlled. But you do it because you don't have the heart for it."

"I've got plenty enough; even to put you in mine for ever."

"It's what I say: you've got a chorus girl's heart. And if not, then show me."

"I'm not going to do anything stupid."

"What a thoughtful youth! You're so well brought up."

"Don't make me angry!"

"Coward! Coward! So, you won't dare come with me tonight?"

"Where? On some crazy adventure?"

"The spinning mill. I'm going to plant a bomb."

"Don't do that."

"I will."

"You'll ruin everything."

"That's even better. I need blood, fire. Death!"

El incendio lo tenía Angustias en los ojos. Parecía que empezaba a arder por allí.

–No se asuste, hombre. A mí me divertirá mucho. El pánico saltará de casa en casa; hará desmayarse a las burguesitas y temblar a esos hombres gordos que salen a pasear por las tardes protegidos por la autoridad y el orden.

–¡Así no se adelantará nunca nada!

–No lo crea, *Gafitas*. Nuestra fuerza está en que todo lo tenemos perdido.

Y luego, con una voz de tañido dulce, una voz que inyectaba en mí el veneno del heroísmo inútil:

–Usted no tiene que hacer nada; acompañarme únicamente.

–En todo caso lo haría yo solo.

–Yo, yo. Quiero para mi vida ese placer. Quiero destruir algo con mis manos. ¿Vendrá usted?

–¡Angustias!

–Ese peligro nos unirá para siempre.

–Iré.

–Gracias. Mañana, a las ocho de la noche, espéreme en el bar del otro día. Vístase de otro modo; como un artesano en domingo.

–Pero hay que preparar la huida.

–Yo me encargo de eso. Hasta tengo dinero.

Estuve a punto de buscar a Pascual Domínguez y contárselo todo. Pero podía más en mí la promesa de Angustias de unirme a su vida con aquel secreto trágico. Además, el solo pensamiento de que ella pudiera considerarme un cobarde y adivinar mi flaqueza interior lubricaba mi ánimo hasta dejarlo propicio al atentado. Sufrí bastante al darme cuenta de que mi espíritu había caído desde la cumbre de las ideas al vórtice de la pasión erótica.

Al día siguiente conseguí de un electricista amigo mío que me prestase su traje y su gorra. Me caractericé delante del armario de mi cuarto como para salir a escena. El traje influyó en mis nervios de tal modo que asistí, casi alegre, al espectáculo de mi propia metamorfosis. Ya no era Carlos Arnedo, alumno de la Escuela de Ingeniería, sino un jornalero anónimo dispuesto a servir la causa sindical. En realidad, me estorbaban el sombrero de fieltro, la trinchera y la camisa de seda para entender la *Teoría de la violencia*, de Sorel. Entonces pensé, no sé por qué, si el alma no será también cuestión de indumentaria.

Aproveché un instante en que el pasillo de la pensión estaba desierto

Angustias had fire in her eyes. It seemed as though it had already started to burn.

"Don't be scared. It will be great fun for me. Panic will fly from house to house. It will make the little bourgeois girls faint and those law-and-order loving fat cats will tremble when they take their evening strolls."

"But it won't further anything, ever!"

"Don't believe it *Specks*. Our strength lies in that we've lost everything."

And then, with a sweetly ringing voice, a voice which injected the venom of useless heroism in me:

"You don't have to do anything; just come with me."

"Whatever, I would do it alone."

"I, I want this pleasure in my life. I want to destroy something with my own hands. Will you come?"

"Angustias!"

"We'll be united for ever by danger."

"I'll come."

"Thank you. Tomorrow night at eight o'clock, wait for me in the bar where we were the other day. Change your clothes; dress like a worker in his Sunday Best."

"But we need to organize a getaway."

"I'll take care of that. I've got money."

I was on the point of searching out Pascual Domínguez and telling him everything. But Angustias' promise to unite our lives with that tragic secret was stronger. Besides, just the thought that she could consider me a coward and guess my inner weakness, fueled my spirit to the point where I was ready to act. I suffered a lot when I realized that my spirit had fallen from the peak of idealism to the vortex of erotic passion.

The next day I arranged for an electrician friend of mine to lend me his clothes and his cap. I dressed for the part in front of the wardrobe in my room, as though going on stage. The clothing affected my nerves to the extent that I almost happily witnessed the spectacle of my own metamorphosis. I was no longer Carlos Arnedo, student of the School of Engineering; rather, an anonymous casual worker, ready to serve the union's cause. In reality, the felt hat, the trench coat and the silk shirt, got in the way of my understanding of Sorel's *Theory of Violence*. Then I had a thought, I do not know why, that the soul could also be a question of clothing.

I took advantage of the moment when the corridor of the rooming house

y me lancé escaleras abajo. Pero no contaba con el portero, apostado en el vestíbulo y dispuesto a ejercer, con el primero que topase, su misión inquisitiva. Dudé si inventar una historia de mujeres para despistarlo o escapar temerariamente a su investigación; opté por lo último y, al verle de espaldas, salí corriendo, mientras detrás de mí rodaba la temible voz:

–¡Eh! ¡Eh! ¿De dónde viene usted? ¡Oiga!

En un taxi fui hasta el bar de la cita.

No eran las ocho todavía; pero ya estaba allí Angustias vestida de obrera... ¿Con un niño en brazos? Sí; con un niño en brazos.

–¡Estupendo, *Gafitas*, estupendo! ¡Ahora sí que es usted de los míos!

–Pero... ¿y ese niño?

–Mi hijito. Véalo.

Me acercó el envoltorio. Era una muñeca enrollada en una manta de lana.

–Para algo serio habían de servir mis muñecas –murmuró Angustias en voz baja.

–¿Y aquello?

–Aquí en la manta. No tengo más que desdoblarla. Pero pesa un horror.

–Tendremos que ir en un taxi.

–Está a la puerta; lo guía un compañero de toda confianza. La fábrica está rodeada de Guardia Civil, que protege a los esquiroles. Yo diré que soy la mujer de uno de los del turno de noche y que necesito hablarle. A usted no le dejarán pasar; pero yo, con el niño, no despierto sospechas. La dificultad está en entrar, prender la mecha y salir antes de los diez minutos.

–¿Cuánto durará la mecha?

–Un cuarto de hora.

–¿De manera que yo...?

–Usted entretiene a los guardias y procura colocarse siempre de modo que no puedan detallar su rostro. Ayer estuve viendo aquello y hay muy poca luz.

Hablaba con una frialdad indescriptible. ¿En qué dramáticas experiencias se había templado el carácter de Angustias para permanecer impasible con la muerte en los brazos? La muerte iba disfrazada aquella tarde de niño recién nacido, y saldría de las entrañas de la anarquista como un monstruo que vomitase devastación y crimen. Pero ¡quién sabe! Quizá aquel hijo tremendo de Angustias, aquel que se mecía sobre su pecho intacto, fuese el Mesías de la humanidad futura.

–¡Vámonos!

was deserted and rushed down the stairs. But I had not counted on the janitor, posted in the lobby and prepared to exercise his inquisitive mission with the first person that he came across. I wondered whether to invent a story about women to throw him off the scent or hastily escape his questioning, but I opted for the latter, and when I saw his back turned, I ran out, while behind me, his fearful voice echoed:

"Hey! Hey! Where did you come from? Hey you!"

The cab took me straight to the bar.

It was not yet eight o'clock; but Angustias was already there dressed as a worker… Did she have a child in her arms? Yes, she had a child in her arms.

"Great, *Specks*! Great! Yes you're really one of us now!"

"But … what about the baby?"

"My little boy. Have a look at him."

I approached the bundle. It was a doll wrapped in a woollen shawl.

"My ragdolls do have a serious use," whispered Angustias quietly.

"And where is it?"

"Here in the shawl. All I have to do is unroll it. But it weighs a ton."

"We'll have to get a cab."

"It's at the door; one of my trusted comrades is driving. The factory is surrounded by the Civil Guard, they're protecting the scabs. I'll say that I'm the wife of one of the night shift workers and I need to speak to him. They won't let you go in; but I won't create any suspicion with a baby. The hard thing is getting in, lighting the fuse and getting out before the ten minutes are up."

"How long is the fuse set for?"

"A quarter of an hour."

"So what about me…?"

"You keep the guards talking and always try to stand where they can't see your face clearly. I was watching that spot yesterday and there's not much light."

She spoke with an indescribable coldness. What dramatic experiences had tempered Angustias' character to make her remain impassive with death in her arms? That night death was disguised as a newborn baby and would come from the entrails of an anarchist, like a monster, vomiting devastation and criminality. But, who knows! Maybe that awesome baby of Angustias, which was swaying on her milk-less breasts, was the Messiah of future humanity.

"Let's go!"

La seguí avergonzado de mí mismo. Porque mientras ella entraba, inconmovible, en el auto, mi sangre se batía como las aguas de dos corrientes opuestas. El coche arrancó sin que ninguno cambiara una sola palabra con el conductor.

A los pocos minutos estábamos en una calle inmediata a la fábrica de hilados. Descendimos, y a los pocos metros apareció la fábrica, jadeante y siniestra. Dos focos eléctricos, como dos alabarderos gigantes, iluminaban la explanada. El edificio parecía haber absorbido las construcciones próximas, porque se levantaba solo y dominante. Más abajo había campo, desmonte, silencio urbano.

Parejas de guardias cabalgaban por los alrededores. Pero no debía de temerse nada porque hubimos de detenernos para dar lugar a que un guardia se acercase, espoleando un caballo somnoliento.

–¿Adónde van?

–A la fábrica. Mi marido trabaja ahí –contestó Angustias.

–Hay orden de que no pase nadie a estas horas –repuso el guardia.

–Es que… Mire usted –dije yo–, la cosa es urgente. Se trata de darle un recado esta misma noche. Porque como hasta el amanecer no deja el trabajo…

–Bueno, bueno. Se lo diré al cabo.

Vino el cabo, que nos increpó con voz agria.

–¿No saben ustedes que por la noche no se puede entrar?

–Es que yo he pasado la tarde fuera de casa –respondió Angustias–, y mi marido se llevó la llave. Ahora no puedo entrar, y el niño…

El cabo contempló un segundo el tierno envoltorio, y dirigiéndose a mí dijo después:

–¿Lleva usted armas?

–No, señor.

–Regístrelo, García.

García echó pie a tierra y me cacheó.

–No lleva nada.

–Bien; pasen ustedes –replicó el cabo–. Esto lo hago bajo mi responsabilidad, ¿eh? No sé cómo salen de casa con niños…

Pero la puerta de la fábrica estaba cerrada. Angustias oprimió el timbre.

–¿Y ahora? –le dije yo en voz baja.

–Ahora preguntamos por un nombre cualquiera.

Salió el ordenanza.

–¿Qué desean?

I followed her, ashamed of myself. Although she got into the car unruffled, my heart was crashing like the waters of two opposing currents. The car set off without anyone having exchanged a word with the driver.

Within a few minutes, we were in a street close to the spinning mill. We got out, and after a few meters the factory loomed, panting and sinister. Two electric beams, like two gigantic halberdiers, illuminated the area. The factory appeared to have absorbed the nearby buildings, because it stood alone and dominant. Further on were fields, clearings, urban silence.

Pairs of guards were riding around it. But we could not let ourselves be afraid of anything as we had to stop to let a guard approach us, spurring a sleepy horse.

"Where are you going?"

"To the factory. My husband works there," answered Angustias.

"Orders are that no one is allowed in at this hour," replied the guard.

"It's that … Look," I said, "this is urgent. It's about getting a message to him tonight. Because he doesn't finish work until the morning…"

"Okay, okay. I'll tell the corporal."

The corporal came and gruffly told us off.

"Don't you know that you can't go in at night?"

"Well I've been out of my house all evening" answered Angustias, "and my husband took the key with him. I can't get in now, and the child …"

The corporal looked at the tender bundle for a second, and addressing me said:

"Are you armed?"

"No, sir."

"Check him García."

García got down from his horse and frisked me.

"He's clean."

"Okay; go on in" replied the corporal. "I'll take responsibility for this. I don't know how you can leave the house like that with a child …"

But the factory gate was locked. Angustias pressed the bell.

"And now what?" I said to her in a low voice.

"Now we ask for any name."

The janitor came out.

"What do you want?"

–Hablar un instante con mi marido, que trabaja aquí.

–¿Cómo se llama?

–Pedro Estévez.

–Bueno; esperen ahí, que preguntaré.

–Oiga, buen hombre. Es que quería darle de mamar al niño, mientras tanto, y aquí hace relente. ¿No podría pasar a cualquier rincón?

El ordenanza vaciló.

–El caso es que no hay permiso... En fin; pasen aquí, al cuarto del conserje, mientras busco a su marido. ¿Dice usted que se llama?

–Pedro Estévez. Es de los nuevos.

En el cuarto del conserje había una mesa, varias sillas y una percha con ropa. Apenas salió el ordenanza, Angustias se sentó, desdobló la manta y sacó una caja alargada con una guita enrollada. La colocó debajo de la mesa y extendió la guita a lo largo de la pared. Yo debía de estar lívido.

–Ahora hay que encender –dijo Angustias.

–Pero ¿y si tarda?

–Nos da tiempo a escapar.

–Gritará y nos echarán mano los guardias.

–Pues hay que encender. Sostén la muñeca.

Sacó del pecho una caja de cerillas y prendió fuego a la guita.

–¿Viene?

–No.

–Pues vámonos.

–No puede ser.

Con espanto vi que la llamita, tan débil, tan insignificante, corría por la cuerda como un gusano.

Angustias me arrancó la muñeca y se plantó en la puerta de la estancia al tiempo que volvía el ordenanza.

–Dicen que ése no trabaja aquí.

–Pues él me dijo que aquí. Será en la otra fábrica.

–Será.

–Muchas gracias. ¡Qué fastidio!

El ordenanza nos abrió la puerta con rostro contrito. A paso largo, sin ver a Angustias, crucé la explanada.

–No corra, por Dios, que es la perdición.

Aún tropezamos con el cabo:

–¿Qué, encontró a su marido?

"To speak with my husband for a moment, he works here."

"What's his name?"

"Pedro Estévez."

"Okay; wait here, I'll ask."

"Hey pal, listen, I'll need to feed the baby in a little while, and it's chilly here. Is there someplace I could go?"

The janitor hesitated.

"It's not really allowed… Well, go on into the janitor's office while I look for your husband. What did you say his name was?"

"Pedro Estévez. He's one of the new ones."

In the janitor's office there was a table, various chairs and a hanger with clothes on it. The janitor had hardly stepped out when Angustias sat down, unfolded the shawl and took out a large box with twine wrapped round it. She placed it under the table and paid it out along the wall. I must have turned pale.

"Now we've got to light it," said Angustias.

"But what if it takes a while?"

"It will still give us time to get away."

"He will shout and the guard will nab us."

"We need to light it. Hold the ragdoll."

She took a box of matches from out of her cleavage and lit the fuse.

"Is he coming?"

"No."

"Right, let's go."

"I don't believe it."

I was shocked to see that the tiny, insignificantly weak flame, was burning down the twine like a worm.

Angustias snatched the ragdoll from me and put it at the door just as the janitor was coming back.

"They say he doesn't work here."

"Well, he said here. Maybe he's in the other factory."

"Maybe."

"Thanks very much. What a nuisance!"

The janitor opened the door with a pained expression on his face. I strode across the forecourt without looking at Angustias.

"Don't run, for God's sake, that'll give us away."

We still bumped into the corporal:

"Well, did you find your husband?"

–Sí; muchísimas gracias.

Yo caminaba automáticamente y llevaba en la nuca el frío de los ajusticiados. Hasta que me derrumbé en el asiento del taxi, que se puso a correr como enloquecido a través de la ciudad. Angustias tiró el envoltorio y abandonó las manos sobre mis hombros.

–*Gafitas*, ahí detrás hemos sembrado la muerte, la justicia. Ya le dimos algo a la idea. Quizá ahora mismo… ¿Vale algo para usted un beso mío?

–No quiero otro premio.

–Pues tómelo.

Y su boca grande y un poco áspera descargó en la mía un beso imponente, eléctrico, rápido y penetrante como un fluido.

–Después de esto, Angustias, doy el pecho, sin temblar, a los fusiles del piquete.

–Se trata de lo contrario. El coche nos dejará en un sitio seguro. Durante dos o tres días permaneceremos escondidos, hasta que las circunstancias digan lo que debemos hacer.

El coche paró en una calle bastante céntrica. Penetramos en una casa que yo no había visitado nunca y allí nos dio de comer una mujer de cabello gris. Más tarde, en una alcoba antigua, Angustias me ofreció la fiesta de sus caricias, una especie de conjunción de amor y muerte. Me dormí muy tarde, agotado. Al día siguiente, Angustias me despertó. Blandía un periódico, rabiosa.

–Una desgracia, Carlos. La bomba no estalló; el ordenanza apagó la mecha. Y, además, lee, lee; la huelga está solucionada. El Comité firma hoy las bases de arreglo.

Mi alma, en cambio, encogida la víspera por el remordimiento, se derramaba de nuevo por todo mi ser como una alegre inundación.

El desastre de Marruecos me llevó al cuartel otra vez. Yo había hecho cinco meses de servicio, comprando el resto por la módica cantidad de dos mil pesetas. Pero al sobrevenir Annual me llevaron a filas para que contribuyese a restaurar el honor de España en Marruecos. Angustias era derrotista y me aconsejaba:

–No debes ir.

–¿Qué remedio me queda?

–Márchate, emigra.

–Ya no es posible. Además, sería un desertor.

–¡Un hombre de tus ideas con uniforme!

–¡No parece sino que el comunismo no tiene ejército!

"Yes; thanks very much."

I was walking automatically, and I felt the cold of the hangman's noose around my neck right up to the moment I collapsed onto the cab seat. It then set off madly through the city. Angustias tossed the bundle away and threw her arms around my shoulders.

"*Specks*, back there, we've sown death and justice. We've already given you some idea what it's about. Maybe right now … Is it worth a kiss from me?"

"I don't want any other reward."

"Well, here goes."

And her generous and slightly rough mouth discharged a powerful kiss; it was electric, quick and penetrating like a fluid.

"Angustias, after that, I'd face a firing squad without flinching."

"To the contrary, the cab was to drop us off at a safe house. We would lie low for two or three days, while waiting for circumstances to dictate our actions."

The car stopped in a relatively central street. We went into a house that I had never seen before and there a gray-haired woman fed us. Later, in an ancient bedroom, Angustias offered me the feast of her caresses, a type of conjunction of love and death. I slept in very late, exhausted. The following day, Angustias woke me. She waved a newspaper, angrily.

"A calamity, Carlos. The bomb didn't go off; the janitor put out the fuse. And what's more, read this, read this; the strike's settled. The Committee is going to approve the basis for the settlement."

Instead, my soul which that morning had been gripped by remorse was again washing through my whole being like a happy flood.

The Disaster of Annual in Morocco took me back to barracks again. I had already done five months of my military service, buying myself out of the rest with the modest sum of two thousand pesetas. But the Annual business called me to the ranks so that I could contribute to restoring the honor of Spain in Morocco. Angustias was a defeatist and advised me:

"You mustn't go."

"What alternative do I have?"

"Go away, emigrate."

"It's not possible now. Besides, I'd be a deserter."

"A guy with your ideas in uniform!"

"You know that even communism has armies!"

–Pero es el ejército de la Revolución.

–Te prometo matar el menor número posible de moros.

–¡Estúpido!

–Pero ¿no comprendes que es imposible?

–A mí no me hables más. Eres un farsante.

Fui al cuartel, naturalmente. Y para acabar de ganarme la antipatía de Angustias hasta me hicieron sargento. El sargento Arnedo instruía a los soldados bisoños en los sagrados deberes de la patria y la disciplina. Cuando en el patio del cuartel, después de la misa reglamentaria, se cantaba «La canción del soldado», el sargento Arnedo sentía una voz interior que le gritaba «La Internacional». Era la voz de Angustias, cargada de recuerdos, mezclada con apasionadas confidencias, que había quedado allí dentro, como el mar en las caracolas. Voz querida y viva, intransigente y soñadora; voz de un mundo imposible, construido con la frágil materia de la imaginación. Y, sin embargo, allí, delante de mí, estaba el pueblo armado, armado por una idea que venía corrompiéndose a lo largo del tiempo en las páginas de los códigos y en las palabras de los hombres.

–¿Qué es la patria? –le preguntaba a cualquier soldado de aquellos que limpiaban su correaje en un rincón.

–Yo… mi sargento, como fui tan poco tiempo a la escuela…

–Tu patria es España, hombre. Claro que si fueras alemán sería Alemania. Ya ves qué fácil…

La mañana que salimos para Marruecos era una mañana de cristal. Como en un vaso aparecía en el horizonte la naranja del sol naciente. Los soldados desfilaban hacia la estación medio encorvados ya por el peso de las mochilas y de las cartucheras. La banda del regimiento tocaba un pasodoble de zarzuela; aquel «Banderita banderita…» encanallado por las gargantas de todas las segundas tiples. Y era espantoso marchar a la guerra entre los compases que horas antes, en las salas de los cabarets, habían servido para envolver las carcajadas de los señoritos calaveras, nietos de aquellos otros que tenían minas en el Rif. De vez en cuando se rompía la espesa formación porque una mujer del pueblo, desmelenada, tendía el almez de sus brazos para rescatar al hijo soldado. Yo miraba las casas mudas, las casas sin dolor, que cobijaban el tranquilo sueño de sus inquilinos. Y veía las otras casas, de ventanas abiertas, de ventanas que eran como ojos atónitos por donde manaba el llanto de la ciudad.

En la estación, según iban subiendo a los vagones los expedicionarios, las damas católicas regalaban escapularios y estampitas. Un teniente, muy

"But it's the army of the Revolution!"

"I promise to kill the smallest possible number of Moors."

"Stupid!"

"But don't you understand that it's impossible?"

"Don't talk to me anymore. You're a fake."

I naturally reported to barracks. And to crown it all, Angustias' dislike of me was made worse because they made me sergeant. Sergeant Arnedo instructed rookies in the sacred duties of country and discipline. When, after church service, *La canción del soldado*[35] was sung on the parade ground, Sergeant Arnedo heard an inner voice calling out *The International*. It was Angustias' voice, filled with memories, mixed with loving confidences, which had stayed there within, like the sea in shells. A loving and living voice, uncompromising and dreamy; the voice of an impossible world, built with the fragile material of imagination. However, there before me, was the nation under arms, armed with a corrupting idea that had gradually come to them through the pages of the Regulations, and by men's words.

"What is Nation?" I randomly asked a soldier, one of those cleaning his webbing in a corner.

"Me …sergeant, I didn't spend long in school, so …"

"Soldier, your nation is Spain. So, if you were German it would be Germany. You see how easy it is…"

We left for Morocco on a crystal clear morning. The rising sun appeared on the horizon like an orange within a tumbler. The soldiers filed towards the station, already half bent under the weight of their packs and cartridge pouches. The regimental band played a popular vaudeville tune; that *Banderita, banderita*,[36] channeled through every cabaret singer's throat. And it was amazing, marching off to war to the rhythms which hours earlier, had served to smother the guffawing, mad-cap young gentlemen, the scions of those other Rif mine owners. From time to time the dense ranks were broken by some wild-haired, local woman offering her tree-like arms in an attempt to rescue her soldier son. I looked at the silent houses, their unfeeling windows sheltering the tranquil sleep of their tenants. And I saw other houses, with open windows, windows which were like agonized eyes from which flowed the weeping of the city.

As the expeditionary soldiers were clambering into their railroad cars at the station; the catholic ladies were giving them scapulars and holy prints.

jovencito, se metía a puñados las imágenes en los bolsillos. A mí quisieron también colocarme un escapulario.

–Señorita, lo siento, pero no creo en Dios.

–Es de la Virgen.

–Ni en la Virgen. ¡Qué le vamos a hacer!

Cuando el tren arrancaba ya, mientras mis amigos me apretaban las manos, yo buscaba entre la multitud el rostro de Angustias. Pero no estaba. El convoy echó a correr entre vivas y sollozos, y yo seguí bastante tiempo en la ventanilla recluido en el camarote de mis gafas. Hasta que los soldados se pusieron a cantar las mismas canciones de los talleres y las eras.

Mi batallón llevaba un año arrastrándose por las pistas de Yebala, desde Beni Ider hasta Tetuán. Guarnecíamos entonces Zoco-el-Arbaá de Beni Hassam, en el camino de Xauen. Yo estaba cansado de dormir bajo las tiendas de lona, de comer huevos fritos en las cantinas y de recorrer los parapetos, apoyando el oído en el pecho de la noche africana. Los periódicos empezaban a hablar de repatriación, y todos, en los soliloquios del campamento, hacíamos planes para la vida futura. Mis camaradas de antes no me escribían, juzgándome, sin duda, un mistificador ideológico. Sólo Pascual Domínguez, comprensivo, me saludaba de vez en cuando con unas líneas llenas de efusión.

Una tarde, me llamó a su tienda el capitán ayudante del batallón.

–Le reclama a usted –me dijo– el jefe de Estado Mayor. Mañana, en la primera camioneta, tradádese a Tetuán y preséntese a él.

Por mucho que reflexionaba acerca de aquella orden, no comprendía su origen. Pensé si se relacionaría con mi antigua intervención en las luchas sociales; pero conociendo los procedimientos militares, donde la primera medida coercitiva es el arresto, deseché enseguida la sospecha. En realidad, aquella inesperada visita a la plaza, después de algunos meses de campo, era una recompensa en la que no había soñado un sargento que no gozaba entre los jefes de ninguna simpatía. Me esperaban el lecho blando, el café de la Alhambra y, sobre todo, Raquel, la hebrea, en su callada alcoba de la Sueca, desde donde oíamos, abrazados, las agudas glosas que el Gran Rabino hacía del Viejo Testamento.

A la mañana siguiente me presentaba en la Alta Comisaría para recibir las órdenes del jefe de Estado Mayor. Un ayudante me hizo pasar entre oficiales de todas las armas, moros notables y comerciantes de la Junta de Arbitrios.

–¿Usted es el sargento Arnedo, del 78?

A very young lieutenant was cramming handfuls of prints into his pockets. They also wanted to give me a scapular.

"I'm sorry miss, but I don't believe in God."

"It's the Virgin."

"Not even in the Virgin. Now, what are we going to do?"

When the train had already started up, and while my friends were shaking hands with me, I was searching among the crowd for Angustias' face. But she was not there. The convoy pulled out to hurrahs and tears, and I remained at the window for quite some time imprisoned in my spectacles' narrow view, until the soldiers began to sing their self-same workshop and threshing-floor songs.

My Battalion was a year hauling itself over the tracks of the Yebala, from Beni Ider to Tetouan. We then guarded Zoco-el-Arbaá de Beni Hassan, on the Chefchaouen[37] road. I was tired of sleeping under canvas tents, of eating fried eggs in the canteens, doing the rounds on the parapets, and of resting my ear on the African night's bosom. The papers started to speak of repatriation, and during all our sililoquies in camp we planned our future lives. My former comrades did not write any more, doubtless judging me, ideologically fraudulent. Only Pascual Domínguez was understanding and greeted me once in a while with some very effusive lines.

One evening, the battalion adjutant, a captain, summoned me to his tent.

"You're wanted", he said to me, "by the Chief of Staff. You are to go to Tetouan tomorrow on the first truck and report to him."

No matter how much I thought about that order, I could not guess at the reason for it. I wondered if it might have something to do with my earlier part in the social struggle; but knowing military procedure, where the first coercive measure is arrest, I immediately dismissed the suspicion. In reality, that unexpected visit to the garrison, after some months in the field, was a reward that a sergeant who enjoyed little sympathy among the officers, could only dream about. What awaited me was a soft bed, the Alhambra Café and, above all, embracing Raquel, the Jewish girl, in her quiet bedroom in the Sueca, where we would listen to the Chief Rabbi's penetrating comments on the Old Testament.

The following morning, I presented myself at the High Commission to receive orders from the Chief of Staff. An adjutant walked me past officers of all the forces, notable Moors and businessmen of the Military Municipal Council.

"Are you Sergeant Arnedo, from the 78th?"

–A la orden de usía, mi coronel.

–Bien. Debe usted presentarse en el hotel Alfonso XIII al coronel Villagomil. Nada más.

–A la orden de usía, mi coronel.

Jamás había oído hablar del coronel Villagomil. Fui al Alfonso XIII, muy intrigado, y pregunté.

–No está en este momento; pero la señora dice que suba.

–¿La señora?

–Sí; viene con su señora.

Metido en el ascensor, yo me preguntaba quién sería aquella familia Villagomil, que con tanto interés se ocupaba de mí hasta recibirme en sus propias habitaciones. Hice una estadística mental de todas las relaciones de mi madre; pero la operación resultó igualmente infructuosa.

El botones me franqueó la cabina:

–Es en el número 35.

Llamé en el número 35. Y de pronto se abrió la puerta y ante mis ojos asombrados apareció Angustias. Pero otra Angustias, transformada por el oxígeno y las pinturas. Tenía el pelo dorado y los labios encendidos por el lápiz reciente. Llevaba una bata esmeralda, abundante como una clámide, y en el índice de la mano izquierda un rubí de color frío.

–Abrázame, hombre, abrázame.

–Pero… ¿qué haces aquí?

–Ya te contaré. Abrázame.

–Bueno. ¿Y si llegan?

- No; si es un abrazo amistoso nada más. Soy –y se puso cómicamente solemne– la señora Villagomil.

–Déjate de bromas y explícame todo esto, porque me voy a poner enfermo de impaciencia.

–Di que le tienes miedo al coronel. Pero siéntate, hombre, en esa butaca… Eso es. Ahora dime: ¿qué tal te va? ¿Eres ya un héroe?

–Soy… Mira: te iba a contestar un disparate. Haz el favor de decirme qué haces aquí y quién es el coronel Villagomil a quien debo presentarme.

–¡Si he sido yo quien te ha llamado! Vamos a ver: contéstame a una sola pregunta y enseguida te lo cuento todo. ¿Tú crees que yo puedo dejar de ser lo que era?

–No lo creí nunca. Sin embargo, todo esto es muy raro…

–Óyeme: llevo en Tánger seis meses trabajando por nuestras ideas. No tuve más remedio que disfrazarme de esto, de lo que fui. Parezco una

"At your honor's orders, colonel sir."

"Good. You are to present yourself to Colonel Villagomil at the Alfonso XIII Hotel. That's it."

"At your honor's orders, colonel sir."

I had never heard anyone speak of Colonel Villagomil. I went to the Alfonso XIII, most intrigued, and asked for him.

"He's not here right now; but his lady says for you to go up."

"His lady?"

"Yes, he came with his wife."

Once inside the elevator, I asked myself who the Villagomil family could be, and why they would be interested enough to receive me in their own rooms. I ran through my entire mother's family in my mind; but the exercise proved equally fruitless.

The bellboy gave me access to their room:

"It's number 35."

I rang number 35. And suddenly the door opened and before my shocked eyes appeared Angustias. But another Angustias, transformed by peroxide and make up. She had golden hair and her lips were aflame with freshly painted lipstick. She was wearing a flowing, emerald bathrobe, and on the index finger of her left hand was a misty-colored ruby.

"Hold me, come on, hold me."

"But … what are you doing here?"

"I'll tell you. Hold me."

"Right. And what if someone comes?"

"Don't worry; this is just going to be a friendly hug. I'm," and she pulled a comically solemn face, "Madam Villagomil."

"Quit joking and tell me what all this is about, otherwise I'll get sick waiting."

"So you're frightened of the colonel. But look, sit down in this armchair… That's it. Now tell me: how are things going with you? Are you a hero yet?"

"I'm … Look: I was about to give you a silly answer. Please tell me what you're doing here and who is the Colonel Villagomil that I've got to present myself to."

"It was me who called you! Let's see: answer me just one question and then I'll tell you everything. Do you believe I could stop being what I was?"

"I never thought you could. But, this is all really strange."

"Listen to me: I've been six months in Tangier working for our ideas. I had no option other than to disguise myself like this, like I used to be. I look

burguesa o una cocota, ¿no es cierto? Ventajas de la edad. Las cocotas de nuestra raza, cuando llegan a los treinta y cinco, no se diferencian en nada de las señoras honorables. Además, yo sabía bien mi oficio. En el hotel de Tánger me hice amiga del coronel Villagomil. Mi labor necesitaba la confianza de un militar de su influencia.

–Pero ¿no eres su mujer?

–Soy… su amante. Sencillamente.

–Y tú, ¿eres capaz?

–Peor para ti si no lo comprendes, *Gafitas*.

–¿Y qué te propones?

–¡Ah! Ésos son mis planes.

–¿Y no puedo yo saberlos?

–Si estás dispuesto a ayudarme, sí.

–No sé de qué pueda servirte, perdido allá en el campo meses y meses.

–Tú puedes observar, enterarte…

–Y eso ¿para qué?

Angustias me auscultó con la mirada el pensamiento.

–¿Sigues creyendo en Lenin, *Gafitas*?

–Sí.

–Pues Lenin está contra el imperialismo burgués, al lado de los pueblos que defienden su independencia, al lado de Abd-el-Krim.

–¡Vamos, tú me quieres adjudicar el bonito papel de espía!

–¿Por qué no? Ése es tu puesto.

–El Partido nada me ha dicho.

–Te lo digo yo en su nombre.

–Pero tú no eres comunista. Tú eres una anarquista individualista; una soñadora que se divierte con el peligro. No, no. Locuras, no.

–¡Tienes miedo! ¡No te importa traicionar las ideas! Todos tus discursos, naturalmente, eran pura palabrería. Querías subir a costa de los trabajadores.

–Eres una insensata.

–Y tú un cobarde, un *patriota*. ¡Qué gracia! Mi patria es la Revolución, ¿sabes? Una cosa más alta, una cosa que no es el suelo ni las fronteras. ¿Qué defiendes con tu fusil? ¿Qué defiendes? Di. A los políticos, a los burgueses, a los curas, a los enemigos del pueblo. Hablas de ver a tu España en los toros y en el fútbol mientras tú y tus piojos os arrastrabais por estas pistas encharcadas.

like a bourgeois or a coquette, isn't that so? The advantages of age. When the coquettes of our race turn thirty-five, there's no noticeable difference between them and reputable ladies. Besides, I knew my job well. In the hotel in Tangier I became friends with Colonel Villagomil. My work required the confidence of a military man with influence."

"But, aren't you his wife?"

"I'm… his mistress. Nothing more."

"And can you deal with that?"

"It will be worse for you, if you can't, *Specks*."

"And what do you propose?"

"Oh! Those are my plans."

"And can't you tell me them?"

"Yes, if you're willing to help me, yes."

"I don't know how I could help you, lost for months and months out there in the bush."

"You can watch, gain information …"

"And what's this for?"

Angustias searched out my thought with her look.

"Do you still believe in Lenin, *Specks*?"

"Yes."

"Well, Lenin is against bourgeois imperialism and is on the side of peoples who defend their independence, on Abd el-Krim's side."[38]

"Come on, you want me to play the charming role of spy!"

"Why not? That's your job."

"The Party has never said anything to me."

"I'm telling you in its name."

"But you're not even a communist. You're a free-spirit anarchist; a dreamer who gets a kick out of danger. No, no. Madness, no."

"You're scared! You don't care about betraying your ideals! All your speeches, of course, were pure words. You wanted to climb up on the backs of the workers."

"You're a fool."

"And you're a coward, a *patriot*. How funny! My country is the Revolution, do you understand? A higher thing, something that isn't about land or frontiers. What do you defend with your rifle? What do you defend? Tell me. The politicians, the bourgeoisie, the priests, the enemies of the people. You speak of seeing your Spain in bull fights and soccer, while you and your lice crawl through these muddy trails."

–Angustias: eres una insensata. Lo de allá poco me importa. Me importa lo de aquí, estos camaradas que se amontonan debajo de las tiendas, sucios, estropeados. Más que una idea vale un hombre. No, no. Yo no seré motivo para que un día caiga uno aquí, y aquí se quede. Llámame lo que quieras; pero esta vez no me convencerás como aquel día de la bomba.

Se abrió la puerta y apareció, sudoroso, el coronel Villagomil. Yo me levanté y me cuadré.

–Siéntese, sargento; siéntese.

Y dirigiéndose a Angustias:

–¡Vaya! Ya lo tienes aquí. Está sano y salvo.

–Y hasta gordo –contestó Angustias–. Le va bien el campo. ¡Qué alegría recibirá su madre cuando sepa que le he visto!

–Si esto es hasta un sanatorio –dijo el coronel–. Los pacos son los que… ¿Usted dónde estaba?

–En el zoco.

–¡Ah! Allí se está bien. Además, Vilar es un buen punto. Vilar manda la brigada, ¿no?

–Sí, mi coronel.

–Tiene pegas de vez en cuando. Pero Vilar…

El coronel Villagomil hablaba a medias. Se le veía buscar las últimas palabras de cada frase inútilmente, hasta que optaba por dejarla en el aire, abocetada. Era gordo y de baja estatura y tenía el bigote blanco y rizado como unas hebras de guirlache. Se desabrochó la guerrera, tatuada de cruces y placas. Angustias le recriminó mientras me miraba de reojo.

–Te vas a enfriar. Aquí tienes la capa.

–Hace calor. Llevo una mañana… de aquí para allá… Ahora resulta que voy a tener que irme.

–¿Adónde? –interrogó vivamente Angustias.

–A la Península. Una comisión.

–¡Qué fastidio! Pues yo me quedo.

–Cuestión de tres o cuatro semanas, creo yo.

Yo no podía disimular mi inquietud.

–Mi coronel, con el permiso de usía, me retiro.

–Quédese a comer con nosotros –dijo Angustias.

–No, no; tengo que incorporarme esta misma tarde. Muchas gracias.

–Usted querrá venir destinado a la plaza, ¿no es eso? –me preguntó el coronel.

"Angustias, you're a fool. That lot matters little to me. Here is what matters, these comrades that crowd in under tents, dirty, messed up. A man is worth more than just an idea. No, no. I am not going to be the reason for one of them getting killed here one day, and being buried here. Call me whatever you like; but this time you won't convince me like you did that day with the bomb."

The door opened and a sweating Colonel Villagomil appeared. I stood at attention and saluted.

"Sit down sergeant; sit down."

And turning to Angustias:

"You see! He's here. Safe and sound."

"He's even put weight on," answered Angustias. "Campaigning suits him. His mother will be so happy when she knows I've seen him!"

"Yes, this is like a sanatorium," said the colonel. "It's the sniping that's … Where are you based?"

"In Zoco."

"Oh! It's alright there. Besides, Vilar is a good 'guy'. Vilar commands the brigade, right?"

"Yes, colonel sir."

"He plays up from time to time. But Vilar …"

Colonel Villagomil only spoke in halves. One could see him looking hopelessly for the last words of every sentence, until he opted to leave them sketched in the air. He was fat and short of stature, and had a white, curly mustache with a crumb-encrusted look. He unbuttoned his tunic, tattooed in crosses and badges. Angustias chided him while looking at me out of the corner of her eye.

"You're going to catch a chill. Here's your cape."

"It's hot. I've spent all day… running here and there… Now it appears I've got to go off."

"Where?' Angustias asked him excitedly.

"To the Peninsula. A mission."

"What a nuisance! Well, I'll stay."

"Question of three or four weeks, I think."

I could not hide my disquiet.

"Colonel sir, with your honor's permission, I'll leave."

"Stay and dine with us" said Angustias.

"No, no; I have to get back this evening. Thank you very much."

"You'd like a garrison posting, is that it?" the colonel asked me.

La proposición era tentadora. Pero recordé mi escena con Angustias y el atrevido designio de aquella mujer que todavía mandaba en mí. Hice un gran esfuerzo:

–No, mi coronel. Quiero seguir en mi batallón.

–¿Usted no es de complemento?

–Sí, señor. Pero están allí todos mis amigos.

–Sin embargo, sin embargo, un destino…

–Me gusta más el campo.

–Bien, bien. Ya lo oyes, Angustias.

Angustias tenía en los ojos tanta ira que de ellos me vino un escalofrío. Pero sonrió:

–Si usted lo quiere… Suerte, pues.

Y me alargó la mano.

–A la orden de usía, mi coronel.

–Adiós. Si quiere algo, ya sabe… Yo…

Me cuadré otra vez y salí. Sin ver a Raquel, sin dormir en lecho blando, con una congoja oscura dentro de mí, regresé al campamento a la hora en que los soldados, cruzado el torso con las mantas a modo de salvavidas, formaban para las guardias de parapeto.

Zoco-el-Arbaá de Beni Hassam. Barracones de titiriteros; tiendas pavimentadas de paja; soldados de gorros azules y rojos alborotando en las cantinas; chilabas parduscas; capotes grises. De vez en cuando un camión, apoplético, camino de Xauen. Blocaos de Audal, de Timisal y Muñoz Crespo. Vosotros sois testigos de que mi vida valía poco entonces para mí.

Por aquellos tajos de tierra amarilla, asido a las crines ásperas de la gaba, con el sol en la nuca como un hacha de fuego, salí con mis hombres día tras día, voluntario de aguadas y convoyes. Por fatigarme y ahogar la voz persistente, opaca, del remordimiento. Mi espíritu era ya un espíritu adaptado y cotidiano, incapaz de apresar el mundo con un ademán de rebeldía. Como los discípulos de san Ignacio, que dejan hecha trizas la voluntad en el cepo de los *Ejercicios*, mi voluntad civil había quedado desgarrada y rota entre los alicates de la disciplina. Me encontraba sin juventud, allí, entre la calígine del campo, frente al Atlas inmenso. Mi juventud no eran mis veinticuatro años victoriosos del hambre y la intemperie. Mi juventud era aquella idea que en otro tiempo me hacía sentirme camarada del africano o del mongol.

It was a tempting proposition. But I remembered the scene with Angustias and that woman's daring plan and the sway she still had over me. I made a supreme effort:

"No, colonel sir. I want to stay with my battalion."

"You're not a reservist are you?"

"Yes sir. But all my friends are there."

"But, but, a posting…"

"I like being in the field more."

"Good, good. You've heard him, Angustias."

Angustias had so much anger in her eyes that I felt a shiver down my spine. But she smiled:

"Yes, if that's what you want… Good luck, then."

And she stretched out her hand.

"At your honor's orders colonel sir."

"Good bye. If you want anything, you know… I…"

I saluted again and left. I did not see Rachel, did not sleep in a soft bed, but I did feel a dark anguish inside me. I returned to camp just as the soldiers, with their blankets crisscrossed over them like lifejackets, were forming up for sentry duty on the parapet.

Zoco-el-Arbaá de Beni Hassan. In the puppeteers' booths are straw-floored tents, and rowdy soldiers in the canteens. Blue and red caps blending with the brownish-gray of the hooded, Moorish gowns and gray military capes. From time to time, an apoplectic truck en route to Chefchaouen. Blockhouses at Audal, Timisil and Muñoz Crespo. You are witnesses to the fact that my life was worth very little to me at that stage.

Through those ravines of yellow earth, grasping the rough esparto grasses on the lower hills, with the sun on the nape of my neck like a flaming axe, I went out with my men, day after day, volunteering for water and convoy details, in order to tire myself and drown that persistent, dull, remorseful voice. My spirit was already a spirit adapted to the daily grind, incapable of capturing the world with a rebellious gesture. Like the disciples of St Ignatius, who leave their shreds of free-will in the spiked belts used in their spiritual exercises; my civilian free-will had been torn and broken among the pliers of military discipline. I found my youth had gone, there among the mist-laden fields, in front of the immense Atlas Mountains. My youth was not my twenty-four years of victory over hunger and appalling weather. My youth was that idea; that idea which in another time made me feel camaraderie with the African and the Mongol. I had renounced the

Yo había renunciado al mejor heroísmo, y me sentía viejo de veras. Porque la vejez no es más que una suma de renunciaciones, de limitaciones, hasta que el espíritu queda transformado en una sombra, en un espectro de lo que fue. La muerte, antes de afectarnos orgánicamente, anda ya como un fantasma por dentro de nosotros.

Zoco-el-Arbaá de Beni Hassam, con sus parapetos erizados de fusiles, su mugre cuartelera y sus coplas babélicas: tú eres testigo de que mi corazón quiso alojar alguna vez la bala enemiga, el pájaro de acero de un paco que llegaba silbando desde la montaña indócil.

Volvimos a Tetuán, ya en otoño. Nuestro corazón viajaba en los topes del tren de Ceuta, en las nubes que venían del lado del Estrecho, en los aviones del correo, en las estrellas que se encendían a la misma hora sobre las calles españolas. Las fuentes del barrio moro llevaban el compás a las guitarras de la alcazaba. Hacer guardia en la plaza, después de tantos meses de campamento, era casi una diversión. Veíamos jugar a las moras en las azoteas y oíamos el español señorial de las judías filtrándose por las rejas de barrotes desnudos.

El único servicio comprometido era el de Casa Osinaga. Casa Osinaga era un puesto establecido fuera del recinto de la plaza. Un comandante había tenido el capricho de construir allí una casa en tiempos de Alfau, suponiéndose, sin duda, capaz de rechazar con su pistola todas las cabilas del contorno. Una noche, como es natural, los moros asaltaron la casa, le prendieron fuego y pasaron a gumía a sus habitantes. Desde entonces se nombraba una guardia de un sargento y ocho soldados para que guardasen las ruinas del edificio, porque no había otra cosa que guardar. Cuando una partida de moros quería sembrar la alarma en la plaza, caía sobre Casa Osinaga y fusilaba a la pequeña guarnición o la hacía prisionera para comerciar después el rescate. Pero parece que el mando tenía interés en demostrar que España no agota fácilmente sus héroes: al día siguiente, otro sargento con otros ocho soldados volvía a Casa Osinaga. Cuando el sargento mayor de plaza, un capitán gordo, benévolo, de grandes mostachos, formaba las guardias, era una escena inolvidable:

–A ver: Casa Osinaga.

–Presente.

El capitán miraba al aludido por encima de sus gafas:

–¿Usted?

–A la orden.

best form of heroism, and I felt truly old. Because old age is nothing more than the sum of renunciations, limitations, until the point where the spirit is transformed into a shadow, a specter of what it was. Death, before it affects us organically, walks like a ghost among us.

Zoco-el-Arbaá de Beni Hassan, with parapets of raised rifles, filthy quarters and babel-like doggerels: you bear witness to my heart once wanting an enemy bullet to lodge within; the sniper's steel bird which would come whistling from the rebellious mountain.

It was already fall, when we returned to Tetouan. Our hearts were traveling in the buffers of the Ceuta train, in the clouds coming from the other side of the Strait of Gibraltar, in the mail flights, in the stars which were shining at the same time above Spanish streets. The fountains in the Moorish district kept in time with the Alcazaba's guitars. To be on guard duty in the garrison, after so many months, was almost fun. We watched the Moorish girls at play on their flat-roofed houses and we heard the Jews majestic Spanish[39] filtering through their bare, grilled balconies.

Casa Osinaga[40] was the only awkward duty. Casa Osinaga was a post established outside the garrison. A major had the fanciful idea of building a house there in the days of General Alfau,[41] no doubt supposing that he would, be able to repel all the tribes in the area with his pistol. One night, as was to be expected, the Moors attacked the house, set fire to it and murdered its occupants with their curved knives. Since then, a sergeant and eight soldiers had been detailed to guard the ruined building, because there was nothing else to guard. Whenever a band of Moors wished to cause alarm in the garrison, they would fall on Casa Osinaga and shoot the small detachment or take them prisoner to ransom later. But it appeared that headquarters was interested in demonstrating that Spain does not easily run out of heroes: the following day, another sergeant with another eight soldiers returned to Casa Osinaga. When the officer-in-charge, a fat, benevolent captain, with a large mustache, formed up the guard, it was an unforgettable scene:

"Let's see: Casa Osinaga detail."

"Present."

The captain looked at the aforesaid over his spectacles:

"You?"

"At your orders."

El capitán hacía un gesto de piedad, como diciendo: «¡Pobre! ¡Quizá no vuelva! En fin, ¡qué ha de hacérsele!». Luego añadía en alta voz:

–Bien, bien; tenga usted cuidado. No duerma. Esta Casa Osinaga...

Y daba un gran suspiro.

A mí no me ocurrió nunca nada en Casa Osinaga. Pero en el cuartel nuevo sí. Allí estaban las prisiones militares: desertores, prófugos, confidentes del enemigo, prisioneros... Me tocó un día de guardia en el cuartel nuevo. Al anochecer, la patrulla de vigilancia llegó para hacer entrega de un preso acusado de intervenir en el contrabando de armas. El oficial me llamó:

–Sargento Arnedo: hágase cargo del detenido y destínele un calabozo provisional.

Salí al cuerpo de guardia. Era una mujer, una señora, oculta por un velo. El sargento de la patrulla me entregó la orden del juez.

–¿Se llama...? ¿Usted se llama?

Y de repente sentí que me ponía pálido, que las piernas no bastaban para sostenerme.

–Me llamo... –dijo la mujer con voz segura y fría–, me llamo Angustias López.

–Angus...

El sargento de la patrulla aclaró:

–Compra armas para los moros. La cogieron esta mañana en el camino de Tánger. Es una *pájara*.

–¡Idiota! ¡Canalla!

El sargento quiso pegarle.

–Aquí no te valen ni el sombrero ni las pulseras, ¿sabes? Habrá que ver de dónde viene todo eso.

Me interpuse:

–Bien. Toma; ya está eso firmado.

Salieron todos y yo le dije a la presa en voz baja:

–¡Angustias! ¡Por favor!

Ella me repudió con un gesto. Y luego, extendiendo sus manos hacia mí, murmuró:

–Toma, toma, traidor, carcelero; colócame tú mismo los grilletes. ¡Eres odioso! ¡Me das asco!

–Eres una loca, una loca...

–Y tú un traidor, un vendido. ¡Ah! Pero yo saldré de aquí, y entonces...

–Calla; te van a oír. ¿Qué hago yo? ¿Qué hago yo?

The captain made a pitying gesture, as if to say: "Poor devil! Perhaps he won't come back! But, there's nothing else we can do with him!" Then loudly adding:

"Good, good; be careful. Don't fall asleep. This Casa Osinaga…"

And he gave an enormous sigh.

Nothing ever happened to me at Casa Osinaga. But in New Barracks, it did. There in the stockade were deserters, fugitives, enemy sympathizers and Moorish prisoners… It was my turn for guard duty one day at New Barracks. As night fell, the guard detachment turned up to hand over a prisoner accused of being involved in arms smuggling. The officer called me over:

"Sergeant Arnedo: take charge of this detainee and place in the holding cells."

I went out to the guard detachment. It was a woman, a lady, hidden by a veil. The sergeant of the guard handed me the judge's order.

"Name…? What's your name?"

I suddenly felt myself turn pale; my legs were giving way.

"My name…" said the woman in a confident and cold voice, "my name is Angustias López."

"Angust…"

The sergeant of the guard explained:

"She buys arms for the Moors. They caught her this morning on the Tangier road. She's a bitch."

"Idiot! Swine!"

The sergeant wanted to hit her.

"Neither your hat nor your bracelets are worth anything here, do you understand? We'll have to see where all this came from."

I interrupted:

"Good. Take it; I've already signed it."

They all left and I spoke to the detainee in a low voice:

"Angustias! For God's Sake!"

She gave me a cold, withering stare. And then, holding her hands out to me, whispered:

"Take me, take me, traitor, jailer; lock me up yourself. You're disgusting! You make me sick!"

"You're crazy, crazy…"

"And you're a traitor, you've been bought. Oh! But I'll get out of here, and then…"

"Shut up; they're going to hear you. What am I going to do? What am I going to do?"

—Morirte de vergüenza. En cambio, yo entro ahí con la frente muy alta.

—¡Calla! ¡Calla!

—¡No me da la gana! He de gritar tu cobardía. Lo sabrán todos, los de aquí y los de allá.

—¡Calla!

Los soldados ya se habían arremolinado a mi alrededor. Si Angustias seguía hablando estaba perdido. Llamé al cabo:

—¡Cabo Núñez! Registre a esta mujer. Encárguese de sus joyas y de su bolso.

El cabo Núñez obedeció.

—¡Canallas!

Ella misma fue entregando las sortijas, los pendientes, las pulseras que dejaron de ceñir su brazo moreno. Luego grité:

—A ver, dos de la guardia, con fusiles: condúzcanla al calabozo número 4.

Así, entre bayonetas, entró Angustias en la celda, desdeñosa, impávida, glacial.

Yo fui ante el oficial de guardia:

—A la orden de usted, mi teniente. La detenida está en el calabozo número 4. He puesto un centinela.

—Pero es una mujer.

—Sí, señor.

—¿Guapa?

—¡Pchs! Regular.

—¿Y qué ha hecho?

—Vender armas a los moros.

—¡Qué curioso! Bien, bien.

Volví al cuerpo de guardia y me desabroché la guerrera porque me ardía el pecho. ¡Tampoco entonces tuve valor para pegarme un tiro!

"Die of shame. Whereas I go in there with my head held high."

"Shut up! Shut up!"

"I don't feel like it! I'm going to shout out your cowardice. Everybody who's around here should know."

"Shut up!"

The soldiers had already begun to mill around me. If Angustias went on talking I was lost.

I called the corporal.

"Corporal Núñez! Search this woman. Take charge of her jewels and her purse."

Corporal Núñez obeyed.

"Swine!"

She was handing over her rings, earrings, and the bracelets which had been clasped to her tanned arm.

Then I shouted:

"Right, two guards with rifles: take her to cell number 4."

And so, a haughty, impassive and icy Angustias entered the cell between bayonets.

I went up to the officer-of-the-guard:

"At your orders lieutenant sir. The detainee is in cell number 4. I've posted a guard."

"But it's a woman."

"Yes sir."

"Attractive?"

"Yeah! Alright."

"What has she done?"

"Sold weapons to the Moors."

"How strange! Carry on, carry on."

I turned back to the guard detachment and unbuttoned my tunic because my chest was on fire. Even then, I did not have the courage to shoot myself!

5

ÁFRICA A SUS PIES

Cuando Riaño no tenía servicio nos reuníamos en su casa del barrio moro a beber té y a fumar kif. Íbamos casi siempre Pedro Núñez, Arturo Pereda y yo. Todos habíamos sido compañeros en los jesuitas, y todos, menos Riaño, estudiábamos carreras civiles cuando se hizo la movilización del 21. Riaño era un muchacho rico, alegre y voluntarioso, recién ascendido a segundo teniente. Para él todo era una juerga: las operaciones, las guardias, el campo o la plaza. Cuando su regimiento salía destacado o en columna, el asistente de Riaño transportaba al carro regimental dos o tres cajas de botellas de buen coñac y otras dos o tres de la cerveza preferida, que iban allí de matute, sin que se enterara el comandante mayor. Luego, en el campamento o en pleno combate, Riaño improvisaba una cantina mucho mejor surtida que las que acompañaban a las tropas. Una vez le arrestaron por llevar a la posición una mujer, con el consiguiente peligro para la disciplina y la moral de la tropa. En otra ocasión sufrió una dura reprimenda del coronel por emborrachar a un prisionero y hacerle faltar a los preceptos coránicos.

Era un buen muchacho, sin embargo, y lo hacía todo con sencillez, poseído de un alborozo de niño. La casualidad nos había reunido, y aunque estaba prohibido que los oficiales confraternizaran con los cuotas, Riaño iba con nosotros a los cafés y al teatro, sin importarle gran cosa tropezar con el jefe de día. Con Pedro Núñez, sobre todo, se llevaba muy bien, porque discutían de fútbol y de caballos.

En cambio, cuando Pereda y yo nos enzarzábamos en una discusión literaria o política, Riaño protestaba:

–Bueno, bueno, camelos. No sé cómo os gusta amargaros la vida con esas cosas.

Pero el orgullo de Riaño era su querida. Su querida le había dado fama en Tetuán, y muchos oficiales jacarandosos palidecían de envidia cuando Riaño, jugando con su fusta, pasaba por la plaza de España con África del brazo. Por aquella fecha Tetuán era un vivero de vicio, de negocio y de aventura. Como todas las ciudades de guerra, Tetuán engordaba y era feliz con la muerte que a diario manchaba de sangre sus flancos. Dijérase que aquellos convoyes silenciosos que evacuaban muertos y heridos, aquellas

5

AFRICA AT HIS FEET

When Riaño was not on duty, we would meet in his house in the Moorish quarter to drink tea and smoke kif.[42] Pedro Núñez, Arturo Pereda and I, almost always went. We had all been companions together at the Jesuits' school, and all, except Riaño, were studying civilian careers until the mobilization in '21. Riaño was a rich, cheerful and headstrong boy, recently promoted to second lieutenant. It was all a party to him, whether on escort duties, on combat operations, or in barracks. When his Regiment was detached or in column, Riaño's orderly transported two or three crates of good cognac and another two or three of his favorite beer on the regimental wagon, smuggled in, without the commanding officer's knowledge. Later, in camp or in the field, Riaño would improvise a much better stock of alcohol than the troops had. He was once arrested for taking a woman up to the position, with the consequent danger to the troops' discipline and morale. On another occasion, he was strongly reprimanded by the colonel for getting a prisoner drunk, and rendering him unfaithful to his Koranic principles.

Nevertheless, he was a good sort; he did everything with ease, and was possessed of a child-like happiness. We had met by chance, and although it was forbidden for officers to fraternize with quota men, Riaño would go with us to the cafes and the theater, without worrying very much about bumping into the duty officer. He got on best of all with Pedro Núñez, because they talked soccer and horses.

However, when Pereda and I got caught up in a literary or political discussion, Riaño would complain:

"Right, right you jokers. I don't know why you like to mess up your lives with those things."

But Riaño's pride was his mistress. His mistress had made him famous in Tetouan, and many a boastful officer paled with envy as Riaño, toying with his riding crop, walked through the Plaza de España with Africa on his arm. At that time Tetouan was a hotbed of corruption and adventure. Like all cities in wartime, Tetouan had happily grown fat, while death daily stained its flanks. One might say that those silent convoys evacuating the dead and

artolas renegridas por la sangre seca de los soldados, eran el alimento de la ciudad. De la ciudad que, mientras se combatía en los blocaos de Beni Arós, mientras los hombres en los parapetos sentían el enorme pulpo del frío agarrado a su carne hasta el alba, jugaba a la ruleta en el Casino y bailaba en la alcazaba con las manos en alto. Pereda le llamaba a Tetuán «la ciudad antropófaga».

La amante de Riaño era una mora auténtica. Aquel lujo no se lo permitían ni los jefes de regulares, que hablaban bien el árabe y tomaban el té con los notables de la ciudad. Más que por sus méritos de guerra se conocía al teniente Riaño por su espléndida querida. Los camareros de los restoranes le llamaban «ese teniente de la mora». Y Riaño gustaba de exhibirla en los paseos de la plaza de España, ataviada con una elegancia francesa, entre el escándalo de las señoritas de la guarnición, unas buenas chicas que volvían de la Hípica como si regresaran de las carreras de Longchamps, o que jugaban al tenis para remedar el lejano Madrid de la clase media. África, con una arrogancia aprendida en dos inviernos de París, no detenía siquiera sus ojos orgullosos sobre aquella asamblea uncida a la música zarzuelera de moda en la Península. Pasaba indiferente, con la mirada por encima de las azoteas, hacia su cabila perdida.

Porque África no se llamaba África; quizá Axuxa o Zulima. Riaño la había conocido en un cabaret de Tánger, recién abandonada por un diplomático de Fez, que acababa de exhibirla en París como una rara planta colonial, hasta cansarse de ella. Por lo visto, África, vestida a la europea, con su cartel galante de mora escapada del aduar, tenía innumerables pretendientes. Nunca supimos por qué había preferido a Riaño, para quien ella sólo era otro lujo de muchacho rico. Sus amigos apenas la veíamos; pero ella estaba viva y silenciosa como un secreto en la casa de amor de Riaño, una casa musulmana que tenía una fuente en el patio. Por detrás de los tabiques había siempre un perfume, un rumor, una presencia misteriosa: África, que iba de la azotea al ajimez y del baño al jardín. A veces, por el frunce de una puerta, veíamos un pijama de seda y una oscura melena de desierto, brillante y salvaje.

Riaño nos contaba que, al principio, África salía a la azotea con sus vestidos europeos; pero las moras de la vecindad la insultaban frenéticamente y la llamaban: «¡Lijud! ¡Lijud!» (judía). Entonces África, para contemplar en paz sus montañas, su Gorgues inaccesible, donde habitaban los pacos mortíferos, para oír al muecín de Sidi Saidi y arrojar todos sus pecados de

the wounded, those wooden saddles that were blackened anew with soldiers' dried blood, were food for the city. While they fought in the blockhouses of Beni Arós, while men on the parapets had their flesh gripped until break of day by the long tentacles of midnight frost, they were playing roulette in the Casino and crazily dancing in the Alcazaba. Pereda called Tetouan, 'the cannibalistic city'.[43]

Riaño's mistress was a true Moor. That luxury was not even permitted to officers of the *Regulares* who spoke Arabic well and took tea with the city's notables. Lieutenant Riaño was famed for his splendid mistress rather than for his war exploits. The waiters in the restaurants called him 'that lieutenant with the Moorish woman'. And Riaño liked to show her off, strolling around the Plaza de España, attired in French elegance, scandalizing the young ladies of the garrison, decent girls who would return from horseback riding as though coming back from the races at Longchamps, or play tennis to mimic the middle classes in far off Madrid. Africa, with an arrogant air, acquired during two winters in Paris, would not even let her proud eyes fall on that group yoked to the cabaret music popular in the Peninsula. She would walk by with indifference, gazing over the roof tops, towards her lost tribe.

Africa was not called Africa; perhaps Ashusha or Zulima. Riaño had met her in a 'cabaret' in Tangier, recently abandoned by a diplomat in Fez, who had just shown her off in Paris like a rare colonial plant, until he tired of her. Apparently, Africa, dressed after the European fashion, was well-known as the Moorish woman who had escaped her village, and had innumerable suitors. We never knew why she had preferred Riaño, for whom she was just another rich kid's luxury. His friends hardly ever saw her; but she was alive and as silent as a secret in Riaño's love nest, a Muslim house that had a fountain in the courtyard. Behind the partitions there was always a perfume, a whisper, a mysterious presence: Africa would go from the roof top to the lattice window and from the bath to the garden. Sometimes, through a chink in the door, we would see silk pajamas and a brilliant, dark, savage, desert mane.

Riaño told us that at first, Africa went onto the flat roof in her European clothes; but the neighboring Moorish women insulted her wildly and called her "Lihud! Lihud!" (Jewess). From then on, she would dress in her tribal clothing, in her wide, thick, cloud-like kaftan, to gaze at her mountains in peace; her inaccessible Gorgues, where deadly snipers lived. While listening to the muezzin of Sidi Saida, she would hurl all her damnable sins out onto

réproba a la ciudad sometida al cristiano, se vestía su traje primitivo, su caftán ancho y tupido como una nube. Sola, con la esclava negra de brazos tatuados, comía África su cuscús y tomaba su té oloroso con el ámbar y la hierbabuena.

–Es a lo que no se acostumbra –solía decir Riaño–, a comer en los restoranes. Prefiere esas bazofias de la cabila. Además, me voy cansando de ella porque es más triste que un fiambre. No sabe más que tenderse a mis pies como un perro.

Pero Pereda descubrió un día los ojos de África acechantes y fríos.

Pereda no era tan ligero como nosotros. Ahora que ya no nos pertenece quiero dedicarle estas palabras:

El soldado de las gafas de concha
Camarada de las gafas de concha, debe de ser alegre estar ya por encima de la vida. Debe de ser alegre no recordar.

Yo descubrí enseguida la fina materia de tu alma, a pesar del traje de caqui o del capote arrugado de tanto arrastrarse por las pistas. Como esos frisos góticos donde alternan las alimañas con los santos, tú eras en la fila de mi sección un dibujo noble y delicado. Con tus gafas de concha, tu cabeza un poco inclinada, tus manos rojas por la presión de la nieve y del fusil. Por eso tu vida se rompió casi sin estrépito como una de aquellas ampollas de cristal de la enfermería que recogieron el último brillo de tus ojos miopes.

–Éste es un maula, una mosca muerta –gritaba el capitán iracundo.

Y es que le hacían daño tu pureza y tu desdén. No dabas importancia a los parapetos, ni a los convoyes, ni al acarreo de piedra, ni a las bárbaras marchas de cincuenta kilómetros. Antes de ir a Marruecos, el capitán te había dicho:

–Usted, que es abogado, tiene que ascender.

Tú le contestaste con voz segura:

–No, señor.

–¿Cómo? ¿Por qué?

–Porque no tengo vocación.

–Pues ha de saber usted –gritó el capitán soliviantado– que la milicia es una religión. Sí, señor (Calderón es un clásico hasta en los cuarteles), una religión de hombres honrados.

Una tarde, los moros atacaban el pequeño puesto de Timisal. El teléfono, angustiosamente, pedía auxilio. Y cuando el capitán pidió voluntarios para una muerte segura, tú diste un paso al frente.

–¿Usted?

the Christian controlled city. Alone with her black slave of the tattooed arms, she ate couscous and drank fragrant tea with ambergris and mint.

Riaño would say, "she's not used to eating in restaurants. She prefers that lousy tribal food. Besides, I'm getting tired of her because she's turned into a complete misery. She only knows how to stretch out at my feet like a dog."

But one day Pereda found Africa's cold and threatening eyes.

Pereda was not as frivolous as we were. Now that he is no longer one of us I want to dedicate these words to him:

The soldier with the tortoiseshell spectacles.

Comrade with the tortoiseshell spectacles, you must be happy as you're already beyond life. You must be happy not remembering.

I quickly discovered your soul's delicate skein, despite your khaki uniform, or your cape, crumpled with so much tramping about on the trails. Like those gothic friezes where vermin alternate with saints, you were a noble and delicate drawing in the ranks of my platoon, with your tortoiseshell spectacles, your head slightly bent; your hands red from the snow and your rifle. Because of this, your life was broken almost noiselessly like one of those glass ampules at the first-aid post which caught the last glint in your myopic eyes.

"You're a good-for-nothing, a phony," the captain angrily shouted.

And your very purity and disdain offended him. You did not care about sentry duty or convoy details, or hauling rocks, or barbaric fifty kilometer route marches. Before going to Morocco, the captain had said to you:

"You're a lawyer; get yourself promoted."

You had answered him confidently:

"No, sir."

"What? Why?"

"Because I'm not right for it."

"Well you've got to learn," shouted the salivating captain "the *milicia* is a religion. Yes sir, (Calderón is a classic even in the barracks) a religion of honorable men."[44]

One night, the Moors attacked the small post at Timisil. The telephone desperately requested aid. And when the captain asked for volunteers for certain death, you stepped forward.

"You?"

–Sí, señor.

Yo corrí a tu lado, enloquecido. Recuerdo tu palidez y tu sonrisa, camarada. Mi dolor debía de empañar tus gafas en aquel instante.

–Pero, hombre, ¿cómo haces esto? Es una barbaridad ir voluntariamente. Hay moros a cientos. Los veo por el anteojo cubrir toda la loma.

–¿Qué más da? Un día u otro...

Y volviste, ensangrentado, en las parihuelas de la ambulancia. Nunca comprenderé tu suicidio, aunque quizá hayas sido tú, entre todos, el que mejor murió por aquella España que sentíamos enconadamente agarrada a nuestro corazón.

Los ojos de África, acechantes y fríos. Riaño era un muchacho sin complicaciones; no se parecía, sin embargo, a otros compañeros que castigaban a sus amantes con el látigo, como si se tratara de un caballo o de un moro de la mehala. África no estaría enamorada de él; pero tampoco tendría razón para odiarle. Los ojos de África tenían el luto de los fusiles cabileños y las sombras de las higueras montañesas. Ojos de esos que se encuentran en un zoco o en una calle de Tetuán y que quisiera uno llevarse consigo para siempre con el mismo escalofrío y el mismo rencor, porque enseñan que hay algo irreparable que hace imperfecta la obra de Dios.

Por aquellos días se combatía en Beni Ider violentamente. Los hospitales de Tetuán estaban repletos de heridos. Todas las tardes cruzaban los entierros por las calles de la plaza. Se decía, incluso, que los cabileños, audazmente, querían penetrar en Tetuán, y se vigilaban los barrios moros de la ciudad donde era de temer una sublevación armada.

Una tarde encontré a Riaño en el café de la Alhambra. Me anunció que le habían destinado a una columna que saldría al día siguiente para reforzar a las que operaban desde el zoco de Beni Hassam. Nos abrazamos con ese abrazo tan particular de la guerra, que es como una despedida más larga.

–Llevarás cantina, ¿eh?

–Espléndida. Ya me aburría por aquí.

–¿Y África?

–¡Bah! La pobre... Pienso dejarle dinero hasta mi regreso.

Y al día siguiente un rumor terrible llegó a nuestro cuartel. Un teniente había aparecido asesinado en su casa. Era Riaño. África le había atravesado el corazón con aquella gumía de empuñadura de plata comprada en Tánger. Y luego, vestida de mora, había huido sin dejar rastro. Sus ojos fríos, desde un ajimez cualquiera, vieron quizá pasar el ataúd a hombros de cuatro tenientes.

"Yes, sir."

I frantically ran to your side. Comrade, I remember your pallor and your smile. My pain should have misted your spectacles right there and then

"But man, why are you doing this? It's barbarous to volunteer. There are hundreds of Moors covering the entire hill. I can see them through my field telescope."

"So what? One day or another…"

And you came back, bloody, on the field ambulance stretcher. I will never understand your suicide, though perhaps it was you, who above all among us, died for that Spain which bitterly gripped our hearts.'

Africa's eyes, watchful and cold. Riaño was an uncomplicated boy; he certainly was not like some of his companions who punished their mistresses with the whip, as though dealing with a horse or a native soldier. Africa was not in love with him; but neither did she have any reason to hate him. Africa's eyes had the mourning of native tribes' rifles and the shadow of the mountains' prickly pears. Like eyes from the souk or a Tetouan street that you might wish to carry away with you forever, bearing that same frisson and that same bitterness; they show that there is something irreparable which makes God's work imperfect.

There were violent battles going on in Beni Ider at that time. The hospitals of Tetouan were full of the wounded. Every night the dead were taken through the fortress's streets. It was even said, that the tribesmen wanted to make a daring foray into Tetouan; the Moorish quarters of the city where an uprising was feared, were watched.

I met Riaño one evening at the Alhambra Café. He told me that he was leaving the next day because he had been posted to a column reinforcing the troops operating out of Beni Hassan. We embraced with that embrace which is so special in war; it is like a much longer goodbye.

"So, you'll be taking your drinks chest?"

"Absolutely. I'm getting bored here."

"And what about Africa?"

"Ugh! Poor kid… I intend to leave her some money until I return."

The following day, a terrible rumor reached our barracks. A lieutenant had been murdered in his home. It was Riaño. Africa had stabbed him in the heart with that silver-handled knife bought in Tangier. And then, dressed as a Moorish woman, she had fled without a trace. Perhaps her cold eyes watched from some lattice window, as the casket passed by on the shoulders of four lieutenants.

6

REO DE MUERTE

Cuando llegamos a la nueva posición, los cazadores estaban ya formados fuera de la alambrada, con sus gorros descoloridos y sus macutos fláccidos. Mientras los oficiales formalizaban el relevo, la guarnición saliente se burlaba de nosotros:

–Buen veraneo vais a pasar.

–Esos de abajo no tiran confites.

–¿Cuántos parapetos os quedan, pobrecitos?

Pedro Núñez no hacía más que farfullar:

–¡Idiotas! ¡Marranos!

La tropa saliente se puso en marcha poco después. Una voz gritó:

–¿Y el perro? Les dejamos el perro.

Pero a aquella voz ninguno le hizo caso, porque todos iban sumidos en la alegría del relevo. Allá abajo, en la plaza, les esperaban las buenas cantinas, los colchones de paja y las mujeres vestidas de color. Un relevo en campaña es algo así como la calle tras una difícil enfermedad. La cuerda de soldados, floja y trémula, desapareció pronto por el barranco vecino.

En efecto, el perro quedaba con nosotros. Vio desde la puerta del barracón cómo marchaban sus compañeros de muchos meses, y después, sin gran prisa, vino hacia mí con el saludo de su cola. Era un perro flaco, larguirucho, antipático. Pero tenía los ojos humanos y benévolos. No sé quién dijo al verlo:

–Parece un cazador, de esos que acaban de irse.

No volvimos a ocuparnos de él. Cada uno se dedicó a buscar sitio en el barracón. Pronto quedó en él un zócalo de mantas y mochilas. A la hora del rancho el perro se puso también en la fila, como un soldado más. Lo vio el teniente y se enfadó:

–¿También tú quieres? ¡A la cocina! ¡Hala! ¡Largo!

Pero Ojeda, un soldado extremeño, partió con él su potaje. Aquella misma noche me tocó servicio de parapeto y vi cómo el perro, incansable, recorría el recinto, parándose al pie de las aspilleras para consultar el silencio del campo. De vez en cuando, un lucero, caído en la concavidad de la aspillera, se le posaba en el lomo, como un insecto. Los soldados del

6

DEATH SENTENCE

When we arrived at the new position, the soldiers were already formed up outside the barbed wire, with their discolored caps and sagging knapsacks. While the officers saw to the handover, the outgoing detachment had fun at our expense.

"You're going to have a good summer."

"Those down below don't throw candy."

"Poor guys, how many sentry duties have you got left?"

Pedro Núñez could only splutter:

"Idiots! Swine!"

The outgoing troops marched off shortly after. A voice shouted:

"Oh, and the dog? We're leaving you the dog."

But no-one took any notice of that voice, because everyone was engrossed in the joy of being relieved. Down there, in the garrison, good bars, straw mattresses and gaily dressed women, awaited them. Being relieved during a campaign is something like being out in the street after a difficult illness. The slack and tremulous line of soldiers quickly disappeared down the nearby ravine.

Actually, the dog stayed with us. It watched from the door of the post as its companions of many months moved out, and then without hurrying, came forward greeting me with its tail. It was an ugly, thin, gangly dog. But it had kind, human eyes. I do not know who said on seeing it:

"It looks like a hunter, like those that have just moved out."

We did not bother any more about him. Everyone was busy looking for a billet inside the post, which soon became a quilt of of blankets and knapsacks. At feeding time the dog got in line, like one more soldier. The lieutenant saw it and got angry:

"You want some too? Get to the cookhouse! Hurry up! Go!"

But Ojeda, a soldier from the province of Extremadura, shared his stew with him. That same night it was my turn for guard duty on the parapet, and I saw how the dog tirelessly went round the compound, stopping at the foot of the loopholes to check the silent terrain. From time to time, a bright spark, fallen in the hollow of the loophole, landed on his back, like an insect.

servicio de descubierta me contaron que al otro día, de madrugada, mientras
el cabo los formaba, el perro se adelantó y reconoció, ligero, cañadas y
lomas. Y así todos los días. El perro era el voluntario de todos los servicios
peligrosos. Una mañana, cuando iba a salir el convoy de aguada, se puso a
ladrar desaforadamente alrededor de un islote de gaba. Se oyó un disparo y
vimos regresar al perro con una pata chorreando sangre. Le habían herido
los moros. Logramos capturar a uno con el fusil humeante todavía.

El practicante lo curó y Ojeda lo llevó a su sitio y se convirtió en su
enfermero. El lance entusiasmó a los soldados, que desfilaban ante el perro
y comentaban su hazaña con orgullo. Algunos lo acariciaban, y el perro les
lamía la mano. Sólo para el teniente, que también se acercó a él, tuvo un
gruñido de malhumor.

Recuerdo que Pedro Núñez comentó entonces:

–En mi vida he visto un perro más inteligente.

¿Recordáis, camaradas, al teniente Compañón? Se pasaba el día en su
cama de campaña haciendo solitarios. De vez en cuando salía al recinto y
se dedicaba a observar, con los prismáticos, las cabilas vecinas. Su deporte
favorito era destrozarles el ganado a los moros. Veía una vaca o un pollino a
menos de mil metros y pedía un fusil. Solía estudiar bien el tiro.

–Alza 4. No, no. Lo menos está a quinientos metros.

Disparaba y a toda prisa recurría a los gemelos. Si hacía blanco, se
entregaba a una alegría feroz. Le hacía gracia la desolación de los cabileños
ante la res muerta. A veces, hasta oíamos los gritos de los moros rayando el
cristal de la tarde. Después, el teniente Compañón murmuraba:

–Ya tenemos verbena para esta noche.

Y aquella noche, invariablemente, atacaban los moros. Pero era preferible,
porque así desalojaba su malhumor. El teniente padecía una otitis crónica
que le impedía dormir. Cuando el recinto aparecía sembrado de algodones,
toda la sección se echaba a temblar, porque los arrestos se multiplicaban:

–¿Por qué no han barrido esto, cabo Núñez? Tres convoyes de castigo…
¿Qué mira usted? ¡Seis convoyes! ¡Seis!

No era extraño que los soldados le buscasen víctimas, como hacen
algunas tribus para calmar la furia de los dioses. Pero a los dos meses de
estar allí no se veía ser viviente. Era espantoso tender la vista por el campo
muerto, cocido por el sol. Una idea desesperada de soledad y de abandono
nos abrumaba, hora a hora. Algunas noches la luna venía a tenderse a los

The soldiers on reconnaissance patrol told me that the next day, at dawn, while the corporal was forming them up, the dog went ahead and quickly reconnoitred the gullies and hills. He did the same every day. The dog was the volunteer for every dangerous duty. One morning, as the water detail was about to go out, he began to bark his head off close to a little bit of low hill. A shot was heard and we saw the dog come back with blood gushing from his paw. The Moors had wounded him. We managed to capture one of them with his still smoking rifle.

The medical orderly patched him up and Ojeda took him to his billet and became his nurse. The incident fired up the soldiers who filed past the dog and proudly talked about his deed. Some petted him, and the dog licked their hands. It was only when the lieutenant also approached him that he gave a bad-tempered growl.

I recall then that Pedro Núñez commented:

"I've never seen a smarter dog in my life."

Comrades, do you remember Lieutenant Compañón? He would spend the days on his camp bed playing solitaire. From time to time he would leave the compound to watch the neighboring tribes through his binoculars. His favorite sport was destroying the Moors' livestock. He would spot a cow or a donkey at less than a thousand meters and ask for his rifle. He would study the shot confidently.

"Up 4. No, no. It's at least 500 meters away."

He would fire then very quickly, get his binoculars. If he hit the target, he would be ferociously gleeful. The tribe's grief at the dead animal made him laugh. Sometimes, we could even hear the Moors shattering the crystal-clear evening with their cries. Then Lieutenant Compañón would murmur:

"We're really going to have a party tonight."

On such nights, the Moors would invariably launch an attack. But it was preferable, because it mollified his bad temper. The lieutenant suffered from chronic otitis which stopped him from sleeping. When the compound looked as though it had been sown with cotton balls, the entire platoon would begin to tremble, because the punishments would multiply:

"Why haven't you swept this, corporal Núñez? Three convoys as a punishment... What are you staring at? Six convoys! Six!"

It was not unusual for the soldiers to look for victims, in the way some tribes do in order to calm the gods' fury. But we had been there two months and had not seen a living soul. It was amazing to gaze out on the dead landscape, baked by the sun. Hour by hour we were overwhelmed by a

pies de los centinelas, y daban ganas de violarla por lo que tenía de tentación y de recuerdo.

Una noche el teniente se encaró conmigo:

–Usted no entiende esto, sargento. Ustedes son otras gentes. Yo he vivido en el cuartel toda mi vida. Siente uno rabia de que todo le importe un rábano. ¿Me comprende?

El perro estaba a mi lado. El teniente chasqueó los dedos y extendió la mano para hacerle una caricia. Pero el perro le rechazó, agresivo, y se apretó a mis piernas.

–¡Cochino! –murmuró el oficial.

Y se metió en el barracón, blasfemando.

Al otro día, en el recinto, hubo una escena repugnante. El perro jugaba con Ojeda y ambos se perseguían entre gritos de placer. Llegó el teniente, con el látigo en la mano, y castigó al perro, de tal modo que los latigazos quedaron marcados con sangre en la piel del animal. Ojeda, muy pálido, temblando un poco bajo el astroso uniforme, protestó:

–Eso… eso no está bien, mi teniente.

Los que veíamos aquello estábamos aterrados. ¿Qué iba a pasar? El oficial se volvió, furioso:

–¿Qué dices? ¡Firmes! ¡Firmes!

Ojeda le aguantó la mirada impávido. Yo no sé qué vería el teniente Compañón en sus ojos, porque se calmó de pronto:

–Está bien. Se te va a caer el pelo haciendo guardias. ¡Cabo Núñez! Póngale a éste servicio de parapeto todas las noches hasta nueva orden.

Una mañana, muy temprano, Ramón, el asistente del teniente, capturó al perro por orden de éste. El muchacho era paisano mío y me trajo enseguida la confidencia.

–Me ha dicho que se lo lleve por las buenas o por las malas. No sé qué querrá hacer con él.

Poco después salieron los dos del barracón con el perro, cuidando de no ser vistos por otros soldados que no fueran los de la guardia. El perro se resistía a aquel extraño paseo y Ramón tenía que llevarlo casi en vilo cogido del cuello. El oficial iba delante, silbando, con los prismáticos en la mano, como el que sale a pasear por el monte bajo el sol primerizo. Yo les seguí, sin ser visto, no sin encargar antes al cabo que prohibiese a los soldados trasponer la alambrada. Porque el rumor de que el teniente llevaba al perro a rastras fuera del campamento saltó en un instante de boca en

desperate feeling of loneliness and abandonment. Some nights the moon came to lie at the sentries' feet, and they felt an urge to rape it just because of the memories it brought back and the temptations it provoked.

One night the lieutenant came up to me:

"You don't get this, sergeant. You are different people. I've lived in barracks all my life. One feels anger because you don't give a damn about anything. Do you understand me?"

The dog was by my side. The lieutenant snapped his fingers and held out his hand to stroke him. But the dog aggressively recoiled and stuck close to my legs.

"Swine!" murmured the officer.

And he went back into the post cursing.

There was a repugnant scene the next day in the compound. There were shouts of delight; the dog and Ojeda were playing around and running after each other. The lieutenant arrived, riding crop in hand, and punished the dog, to such an extent that the stripes were marked with blood on the animal's skin. Ojeda, very pallid, trembling a little under his shabby uniform, complained:

"This…isn't good, Lieutenant, sir."[45]

Those of us who witnessed this were terrified. What would happen next? The officer was furious:

"What did you say? Stand at attention! At attention!"

Ojeda fearlessly held his gaze. I do not know what Lieutenant Compañón saw in his eyes, but he suddenly calmed down.

"That's fine. You're going to go gray on guard duty. Corporal Núñez! Put him on sentry duty every night until you hear otherwise."

Very early one morning, Ramón the lieutenant's orderly, captured the dog on his orders. The kid was a fellow provincial of mine and he brought me the news straight away.

"He's told me to bring him one way or another. I don't know what he wants to do with him."

Shortly after, the two of them left the post with the dog, being careful not to be seen by the other soldiers that were not on duty. The dog resisted that strange walk and Ramón almost had to carry him in the air by the collar. The officer went in front, whistling, with his binoculars in his hand, like someone who is going for a walk downhill as the sun begins to rise. I followed them without being seen, but not before ordering the corporal not to let the soldiers cross the barbed wire. The rumor that the lieutenant was dragging the dog away from the post instantly went from mouth to mouth. I

boca. Pido a mis dioses tutelares que no me pongan en trance de presenciar otra escena igual, porque aquélla la llevo en mi memoria como un abismo. Los dos hombres y el perro anduvieron un buen rato hasta ocultarse en el fondo de una torrentera. Casi arrastrándome, para que no me vieran, pude seguirlos. La mañana resplandecía como si tuviese el cuerpo de plata. De la cabila de allá abajo subía un cono de humo azul, el humo de las tortas de aceite de las moras. Yo vi cómo el oficial se desataba el cinto y ataba las patas del tierno prisionero. Vi después brillar en sus manos la pistola de reglamento y al asistente taparse los ojos con horror. No quise ver más. Y como enloquecido, sin cuidarme siquiera de que no me vieran, regresé corriendo al destacamento, saltándome la sangre en las venas como el agua de las crecidas.

Media hora después regresaron, solos, el oficial y el soldado. Ramón, con los ojos enrojecidos, se acercó a mí, temeroso.

–Sargento Arnedo... Yo, la verdad...

–Quita, quita. ¡Pelotillero! ¡Cobarde!

–Pero ¿qué iba a hacer, mi sargento?... No podía desobedecerle. Bastante vergüenza tuve. Dio un grito, sólo uno.

Me marché por no pegarle. Pero lo de Ojeda fue peor. Desde la desaparición del perro andaba con los ojos bajos y no hablaba con nadie. Merodeaba por los alrededores de la posición expuesto al paqueo. Un día apareció en el recinto, entre una nube de moscas, con el cadáver del perro, ya corrompido, en brazos. Pedro Núñez, que estaba de guardia, tuvo que despojarle violentamente de la querida piltrafa y tirar al barranco aquel montón de carne infecta.

beg my guardian angels never to put me through such a scene again, because I carry it like an abyss in my memory. The two men and the dog went quite a way until they were lost to sight at the bottom of a waterfall. Only by almost dragging myself along, was I not seen by them. The morning shone forth as though clad in a silver body. From the tribe down below rose a cone of blue smoke, the smoke of the Moors' olive oil cakes. I watched as the officer took off his belt and tied up the prisoner's soft paws. I then saw his service pistol glint in his hands, and his orderly cover his eyes in horror. I did not want to see more. And like someone crazy, without worrying whether they had seen me or not, I ran back to the post, with blood spurting through my veins like a river in spate.

Half an hour later the officer and the soldier came back, alone. Ramón, with reddened eyes, timidly came up to me.

"Sergeant Arnedo... I, the truth is…"

"Leave it, leave it. Brown nose! Coward!"

"But sergeant, what could I do?...I couldn't disobey him. I'm ashamed enough. He cried out, just once."

I walked off; otherwise I would have hit him. But it was worse for Ojeda. Since the dog's disappearance he had been walking around with his eyes lowered, not speaking to anyone. He would loiter around parts of the post that were exposed to sniper fire. One day, he appeared in the compound, amid a cloud of flies with the dog's already rotten body in his arms. Pedro Núñez, who was on guard duty, had to violently snatch away his beloved wretch and hurl that mountain of rotten flesh into the gully.

7

CONVOY DE AMOR

Esto no me ha sucedido a mí, porque a mí no me han pasado nunca cosas extraordinarias; pero le ocurrió a Manolo Pelayo, que estuvo a punto de ir a presidio por aquello. Desde entonces, Manolo Pelayo habla con un gran odio de las mujeres y pasea su celibato melancólico por las salas desiertas del Casino.

–Son la perdición... Son la perdición... –suele murmurar, con la cabeza apoyada en los cristales de la galería.

Por el paseo de enfrente cruzan las parejas de novios, guillotinadas por el crepúsculo. Manolo Pelayo, cuando se cansa de los divanes del Casino, se va al monte, a la caza de la perdiz o del jabalí. Allí permanece semanas enteras. Luego hemos sabido que, además de la cinegética, practica en la montaña el ejercicio sexual. Pero sin entusiasmo, como una jornada viril inevitable, deseando que todo se haga en el menor tiempo posible. Parece que las campesinas del contorno están maravilladas de aquel señorito huraño, al que reciben en el pajar o en la cuadra, en silencio y a oscuras, después de ajustar la entrevista con el criado. Para algunas es un arcángel violento, que lleva el ardiente dardo de la anunciación. Lo conduce la noche y en la noche se pierde, como un milagro atroz y dulce a la vez.

Manolo Pelayo fue cabo de un batallón expedicionario. Su sección estaba destacada en un puesto avanzado de Yebala. Hacía convoyes al zoco con frecuencia y alguna vez tuvo agresiones de importancia. Lo que voy a contar es mil veces más espantoso que un ataque rebelde. Al fin y al cabo, la guerra es una furia ciega en la cual no nos cabe la mayor responsabilidad. Un fusil encuentra siempre su razón en el fusil enemigo.

Pero esto es otra cosa, una cosa repugnante y triste.

Para comprenderlo hay que haber padecido a los veintitrés años la forzosa castidad de un campamento. Se remueven todas las escorias del instinto y emanan un vaho corrompido de sueños impuros, de bárbaras tentaciones, de angustias perennes. Ni la sed ni el hambre mortifican tanto como esta rebelión de la carne forzada por el recuerdo y la fantasía. El alma se mezcla también en el clamor físico, azuza los sentidos como un cómplice cobarde y astuto. A veces, la nostalgia tierna del atardecer, el terror de la noche, la

7

LOVE'S CONVOY

This did not happen to me, because nothing extraordinary has ever happened to me; but it did happen to Manolo Pelayo, who was on the point of being sent to the penitentiary for it. Since then, Manolo Pelayo talks about women with huge loathing and whiles away his melancholic celibacy in the Casino's empty halls.

"They're our undoing... They're our undoing..." he mutters, with his head resting on the glass balustrade.

On the sidewalk in front, young couples pass by, guillotined by the twilight. When Manolo Pelayo tires of the Casino's couches, he goes hunting ptarmigan and wild boar in the mountains. He stays there for whole weeks. Later, we found out that, besides hunting in the mountains, he partook of sexual exercise. But unenthusiastically, like an inevitable masculine chore; wanting everything to be over in the shortest possible time. It appears that the peasant girls in the area are astonished by that moody, young, rich kid, whom they receive in the hay loft or in the stable, silently and in darkness, after arranging a tryst through his servant. To some, he is a violent archangel, who carries the burning dart of annunciation. He is driven by the night and in the night he loses himself, at once like an appalling, yet sweet, miracle.

Manolo Pelayo was a corporal in an expeditionary Battalion. His platoon was deployed to an advance post in Yebala.[46] He often took part in convoys to Zoco and sometimes he was involved in major battles. What I am about to relate is a thousand times more shocking than a rebel attack.[47] All in all, war is blind fury and the greatest responsibility for it does not lie with us. A rifle always finds its justification in the enemy's rifle.

But this is something else, a sad and repugnant thing.

To understand it you need to have experienced at the age of twenty-three, the forced chastity of life in camp. All the dregs of instinct are stirred up and give off a corrupted vapor of impure dreams, of barbarous temptations, of perennial anguish. Neither thirst nor hunger torment so much as this rebellion of the flesh, forced by memory and fantasy. The soul also mixes in with the physical outcry and inflames the emotions like a cunning, cowardly accomplice. At times, the sweet nostalgia of twilight, the terror of the night,

misma voz de la tierra distante, no son sino olas de lujuria coloreadas por el alma en vigilia. También de modo semejante vierte el cielo sus tintas en el mar.

El batallón de Manolo Pelayo llevaba siete meses en el campo. Siete meses en una posición pequeña, en uno de aquellos puestos perdidos, donde de repente le entra a uno el temor de que se han olvidado de él en las oficinas del mando. Cuando cada quince días llegaba al zoco aquel convoy, todos íbamos a verlo para cotejar nuestro aspecto con el de aquellos soldados rotos, consumidos y mustios. A su lado, nosotros éramos casi felices, con nuestras cantinas bien surtidas, nuestros periódicos de tres fechas y nuestros moros tranquilos que nos vendían a diario la fruta y la caza.

Una tarde, a la llegada de la camioneta de Tetuán, el zoco se alborotó con la presencia de una mujer. De una señora rubia y alegre, muy joven, que dejaba un rastro de perfumes. Todo el campamento se estremeció. Cada hombre era un nervio cargado de escalofríos voluptuosos. Los soldados salían a la puerta de los barracones, se subían a los muros de la explanada, corrían de un lado a otro, atropellándose para verla. Ella iba sembrando el escándalo de su juventud entre aquella chusma hambrienta, desorbitada y torva, que sentía al unísono el bárbaro acezar de la lujuria. Era asombroso cómo se abría paso la mujer entre la fronda de obscenidades, a la manera del sol en una floresta salvaje. Y su aroma quedaba quieto y denso en la pista, como si el aire fuera una vasija dispuesta para guardarlo. Yo vi aquel día a muchos compañeros míos aspirar fuerte el vapor de la viajera y tenderse después en la paja de la tienda, a solas con aquella fragancia, mareados deliciosamente por ella como por una droga.

La mujer rubia, con el sargento que la había acompañado desde Tetuán, penetró en la oficina del jefe de la posición. El jefe era el coronel Vilar, un hombre locuaz y alegre que en vísperas de operaciones, mientras los oficiales discutían de táctica y estrategia, ilustraba los mapas del Estado Mayor con dibujos obscenos. En aquel momento estaba de tertulia con el ayudante y el capellán. Al ver a la mujer, los tres se levantaron. El coronel Vilar, erguido, sonriente, no pudo menos de retorcerse el bigote entrecano.

—Mi coronel —anunció el sargento—: se trata de la esposa del teniente López, el de Audal. Trae una carta del alto comisario para usía.

—Sí, señor —dijo ella, adelantándose con un sobre en la mano—; el general es amigo mío.

—¡Ah!

the same voice from a distant land, are nothing more than waves of lust tinged by the sleepless soul. Similarly, the heavens also pour their colors onto the sea.

Manolo Pelayo's Battalion had been in the field for seven months. Seven months in a small post, in one of those lost positions, where suddenly you start to fear that they have forgotten about you at their desks at headquarters. When that convoy arrived from Zoco every two weeks, we all went out to look at it in order to compare our appearance with those broken, worn out and withered soldiers. Next to them, we were almost happy, with our well-stocked canteens, our fairly current newspapers and our peaceful Moors who daily sold us fruit and game.

One afternoon, when the small truck from Tetouan arrived, the Zoco was excited by the presence of a woman. She was a very young, happy, blonde, who spread a waft of perfume as she went. The entire camp trembled. Every man turned into a nerve filled with lustful fevers. Soldiers came out from the doors of their huts and climbed up onto the walls of the compound. They ran from one side to the other, tripping over themselves to see her. She was sowing the scandal of her youth among that baleful, hungry, disorientated rabble, who in unison felt the barbarous panting of lust. It was amazing how the woman opened her way through the foliage of obscenities, like the sun in a wild forest. Her scent remained on the track, dense and undisturbed, as if the air were a vessel ready to hold it.[48] That day I saw many of my comrades deeply breathe in the visitor's vapors and then lie down on their straw filled bunks, alone with that fragrance, in a deliciously dizzied drug-like trance.

The blonde woman, with the sergeant who had accompanied her from Tetouan, entered the post commander's office. The officer in charge was colonel Vilar, a cheerful, garrulous man who on the eve of operations, while his officers discussed tactics and strategy, would decorate the General Staff's maps with obscene sketches. At that moment, he was chatting with his adjutant and the chaplain. Upon seeing the woman, the three men stood up. Colonel Vilar, upright and smiling, could only twirl his grayish mustache.

"Colonel sir," said the sergeant. "It's the wife of Lieutenant López, the one at Audal. She's brought a letter from the High Commissioner for your honor. "

"Yes sir," she said, going forward with an envelope in her hand; "the general's a friend of mine."

"Ah!"

Pero después de aquel ¡ah! exhalado en tono de suspiro, al coronel le
costaba trabajo dejar de mirar a la recién llegada para leer la carta. Ella
entonces se quitó el sombrero:

–¿Puedo quitarme el sombrero? Hace tanto calor...

–Quítese lo que quiera –exclamó el coronel–. Una mujer como usted
manda siempre.

–Gracias... Vilar.

–Vi... Vilar. ¿Sabe usted mi apellido?

–¡Ay, qué gracia! ¡Pues claro! Y su nombre también: don Manuel. ¡Manolo!

–Eso, eso: Manolo. ¿De dónde nos conocemos, pues?

–¡Si lo dice el sobre!

El ayudante y el capellán se miraban asombrados. Al capellán, sobre todo,
se le presentía desgranando mentalmente las sílabas de aquel «¡Manolo!»
lanzado con tanta desenvoltura por la viajera. El sargento no sabía qué hacer:

–Mi coronel, yo...

–Sí, hombre, márchese.

Y luego, dirigiéndose a la mujer:

–Está usted muy bien así, sin sombrero.

–¿De verdad?

Estaba bien, muy bien. El pelo, libre, era un remolino de fuego. Toda ella
estaba un poco sofocada.

–Estoy ardiendo. Mire usted este brazo. Lo tengo rojo. Arde.

El coronel se acercó tanto que ella tuvo que retirarse.

–Es verdad; arde.

El capellán dio un respingo ante el brazo desnudo:

–Mi coronel, si usted no me manda nada...

–Nada, nada. Hasta luego.

Al ayudante, miope, también le interesaba, por lo visto, aquel brazo
ardiente y oloroso, porque no demostraba ninguna prisa por marcharse.

–Siéntese usted. Aquí hay una silla. Poco cómoda, porque en campaña...
Siéntese usted, Carmen. Carmela, ¿no es eso?

–Eso es. Un nombre de morena dicen que es el mío. Ya ve usted, tan
rubia...

–Pero usted es muy atrevida, Carmela. Venir así, sola, sin miedo al
paqueo. ¡Mucho debe de querer a su marido!

–¡Huy! Muchísimo. Hace un año que no nos vemos. Yo me dije: «¡Pues
cuando los moros no le han hecho a él nada, que se mete con ellos, no me
van a matar a mí, que no pienso hacerles daño!».

But after that 'ah!' breathed as a sigh, it was hard for the colonel to stop looking at the recent arrival in order to read the letter. She then took off her hat:

"May I take off my hat? It's so hot …"

"Take off whatever you want," exclaimed the colonel. "For a woman like you, I'm always yours to command."

"Thank you…Vilar."

"Vi… Vilar. You know my name?"

"Oh, how funny! Well of course! And your first name too: Manuel. Manolo!"

"That's right: Manolo. Where do we know each other from?"

"It says it on the envelope!"

The adjutant and the chaplain looked at one another in amazement. The chaplain, above all, was mentally separating the syllables of that 'Manolo!' said so confidently by the traveler. The sergeant did not know what to do:

"Colonel sir, I…"

"Yes, man, dismissed."

And then, addressing the woman:

"You're really fine like that, hatless."

"Really?"

She was fine, quite fine. Her hair, now freed, was like a whirlpool of fire. But she was sweltering.

"I'm burning up. Look at my arm. It's red. It's burning."

The colonel went so close, that she had to draw back.

"It's true; you're burning."

The chaplain gave a start at the bare arm:

"Colonel, if you don't need me for anything…"

"Nothing, nothing. I'll see you later."

The myopic adjutant also appeared to be interested in that fragrant, burning arm, because he showed no sign of leaving.

"Sit down. Here's a chair. It's not very comfortable, because on campaign… Sit down, Carmen. Or is it Carmela?"

"That's it. It's a name suggestive of a brunette, at least that's what they say. As you can see, I'm so blonde…"

"But you're very plucky Carmela. Coming here all on your own and not being afraid of snipers. You must love your husband a lot!"

"Oh! Very much. We haven't seen each other for a year. I said to myself, 'well, he's meddled with the Moors and they haven't done anything to him; they aren't going to kill me, as I'm not planning on hurting them!'"

–Sin embargo, sin embargo… Audal es un destacamento avanzado, a tres horas de camino, monte arriba.

–Además –objetó el ayudante–, allí no hay sitio para alojar a una mujer. Un barracón pequeño, sucio…

Pero Carmela no se arredraba:

–Es igual. A mí me encantan estas dificultades. Lo mismo me decía el general en Tetuán. Pero se me ha metido este viaje en la cabeza… ¡Ay! Me figuro la sorpresa de Pepe: «¿Tú aquí? ¿Tú aquí? ¡Loca! ¡Loca!». Y luego los abrazos, ¿sabe usted? ¡Qué sorpresa!

El coronel la escuchaba con la boca abierta:

–Bien, bien. Pues, nada; irá usted a Audal.

Y luego, dirigiéndose al ayudante:

–Ramírez, haga el favor de avisar al cabo del convoy de Audal que se presente a mí. Y que ensillen un mulo para Carmela.

–Perfectamente, mi coronel.

El ayudante, distendidas las aletas de la nariz por el perfume de Carmela, salió para cumplir la orden.

El cabo Pelayo se presentó en la oficina del coronel, con correaje y fusil. A pesar del uniforme descolorido por el agua y el sol, el cabo Pelayo tenía un aspecto agradable. Era un muchacho fuerte y distinguido, en el cual las privaciones de la campaña no habían dejado huella deprimente; al contrario, se le notaba enjuto y ágil como un deportista. Al entrar le recibieron los ojos de Carmen, que en aquel momento comenzaron a gravitar sobre él como cuerpos celestes.

–Usted es el cabo de Audal, ¿no es eso?

–Sí, mi coronel.

–¿Cuánto tiempo tarda en llegar el convoy?

–Unas dos horas.

–Unas dos horas. Bien. Usted hace con frecuencia este servicio…

–Cada quince días. Hace siete meses que estamos destacados.

–Perfectamente. Esta señora irá con ustedes. Es la esposa del teniente. Usted me responde de ella con la cabeza. ¿Lo oye usted? Con la cabeza.

–Sí, mi coronel.

–¡Por Dios, Vilar! ¡Que yo no valgo tanto! –intervino Carmen, risueña–. ¡Pobre chico!

"Quite but… Audal is an advance post, three hours by road, up the mountain."

"Besides,' objected the adjutant, 'there's nowhere there for a woman to stay. A small, dirty hut…"

But Carmela was not put off:

"It's not a problem. The general in Tetouan said the same thing but difficulties like this delight me. And I can't get this visit out of my head… Oh! Imagine Pepe's surprise:

'You, here? You, here? You're crazy! Crazy!' And then the embrace, you know? What a surprise!"

The colonel listened open-mouthed:

"Fine, fine. Well, that's it; you're going to Audal."

And then, addressing his adjutant:

"Ramírez, please advise the corporal in charge of the Audal convoy to present himself to me. And order a mule to be saddled for Carmela."

"Of course, colonel."

The adjutant, nostrils distended by Carmela's perfume, left to do the colonel's bidding.

Corporal Pelayo reported to the colonel's office, with webbing and a rifle. In spite of his uniform, which was bleached by sun and rain, Corporal Pelayo had a pleasant appearance. He was a strong and distinguished looking boy, the hardships of the campaign had not left any dispiriting marks; quite the opposite, he looked lean and agile like a sportsman. On entering he met Carmen's eyes, which at that moment had begun to gravitate towards him like celestial bodies.

"You're the Audal corporal, aren't you?"

"Yes, colonel sir."

"How long does it take the convoy to get there?"

"Some two hours."

"Some two hours. Good. You often do this duty…"

"Every two weeks. We've been deployed for seven months."

"Excellent. This lady will go with you. She's the lieutenant's lady. If anything happens to her your head will roll… Do you hear me? Your head will roll."

"Yes, colonel sir."

"Goodness me, Vilar! I'm not worth that much!" Carmen interjected with a smile. "Poor boy!"

—Usted dispondrá la fuerza —siguió diciendo el coronel— de modo que esta señora vaya protegida mejor que nada. Mejor que el saco de los víveres. Con eso está dicho todo.

—Sí, mi coronel.

—Puede retirarse. ¡Ah! Cuando el convoy esté preparado, avíseme.

Minutos después el convoy de Audal estaba en la carretera, dispuesto a partir. Lo componían el cabo, seis soldados, dos acemileros y dos mulos. En uno de éstos se habían colocado una jamuga para Carmen, que llegó con el coronel entre una doble fila de ojos anhelantes. El coronel la ayudó a subir a la cabalgadura, sosteniendo en su mano, a manera de estribo, el pie pequeño y firme. Fue aquél un instante espléndido e inolvidable, porque, por primera vez y en muchos meses, los soldados del zoco vieron una auténtica pierna de mujer, modelada mil veces con la cal del pensamiento. Ya a caballo, Carmen repartía risas y bromas sobre el campamento, sin pensar que sembraba una cosecha de sueños angustiosos. Diana refulgente sobre la miseria de la guerra, en lo alto de un mulo regimental, mientras los soldados la seguían como una manada de alimañas en celo, Carmen era otra vez la Eva primigenia que ofrecía, entre otras promesas y desdenes, el dulce fruto pecaminoso.

Aquellos hombres se custodiaban a sí mismos. Porque, de vez en cuando, la falda exigua descubría un trozo de muslo, y algún soldado, sudoroso y rojo, exhalaba un gruñido terrible.

El sol bruñía la montaña y calcinaba los pedruscos. Al cuarto de hora de camino, Carmen pidió agua. El cabo le entregó su cantimplora y ella bebió hasta vaciarla.

—¡Qué calor, Dios mío! ¿Falta mucho?

—¡Huy, todavía!…

Le cayeron unas gotas en la garganta y ella bajó el escote para secarse. Pelayo sintió que la sangre le afluía a las sienes como una inundación.

Al devolverle la cantimplora, Carmen le rozó los dedos con su mano. Y Manolo Pelayo estuvo a punto de tirar el fusil y detener al mulo por la brida, como los salteadores andaluces.

—Usted será soltero, ¿verdad? —le dijo Carmen.

—Sí, señorita.

—¿Con novia?

—¡Bah! Tanto tiempo lejos… Ya no se acuerdan.

—¡Qué ingratas! Un muchacho tan simpático…

—Muchas gracias.

"You arrange the convoy," the colonel continued, "so that this lady has the utmost protection. Even better than the food supplies and that says it all."

"Yes, colonel sir."

"Dismissed. Oh! When the convoy's ready, inform me."

Minutes later the Audal convoy was on the road, ready to leave. It was composed of the corporal, six soldiers, two muleteers and two mules. A special saddle had been put on one of them for Carmen, who arrived with the colonel between a double file of eager eyes. The colonel helped her mount, using his hand as a stirrup to support her small, firm foot. That was a wonderful and unforgettable moment, because for the first time in many months, the soldiers at Zoco saw a real woman's leg, modeled a thousand times in their imaginations. Already mounted, Carmen shed banter and laughter over the camp, without realizing that she was sowing a harvest of anguished dreams. Diana resplendent above the misery of war, high up on a regimental mule, while the soldiers followed her like a pack of animals on heat, Carmen was again the original Eve, with tantalizing promises and the expectation of sweetly sinful fruits.

Those men had to control themselves. Because from time to time, her flimsy skirt showed a flash of thigh, and a sweaty, red-faced soldier would let out a terrible groan.

The sun burnished the mountain and scorched the rough rocks. After being on the road for a quarter of an hour, Carmen asked for water. The corporal gave her his canteen and she drank it dry.

"My God, it's so hot! Is there far to go?"

"Oh, quite some way!..."

A few drops fell onto her cleavage and she lowered her neckline to dry them off. Pelayo felt the blood rush to his temples like a flood.

On giving back the canteen, Carmen brushed his fingers with her hand. And Manolo Pelayo was on the point of throwing away his rifle and pulling the mule to a halt by its bridle, like an Andalusian highwayman.

"You must be single, right?" Carmen said to him.

"Yes, miss."

"Do you have a girl?"

"Uh! A long time ago... They don't remember."

"How ungrateful! You're such a nice boy..."

"Thank you very much."

–Y éstos ¿tienen novia?

–Aquél y éste –dijo señalando a dos de los soldados– sí la tienen. Oye, López, ¿cómo se llama tu novia?

–Adela.

–Bonito nombre –declaró Carmen–. Será muy guapa.

–Sí... Pero usted es más.

Y López acompañó el piropo de una carcajada metálica, casi obscena.

–Eres muy galante, López –replicó la viajera–. Que no lo sepa Adela.

–Es que yo... Verá usted... Yo...

Pero a López debía de ocurrírsele una barbaridad, porque, de pronto, se quedó muy serio, prendido en los labios de Carmen, como un moscardón en un tarro de miel.

El calor era asfixiante. La pista era ahora una pendiente callosa, sin un árbol, ni una hierba, ni un pájaro. Los mulos ascendían trabajosamente en zigzag.

–Cabo –exclamó Carmela–, ¿a que no sabe usted lo que me gustaría ahora?

–No sé.

–Tirar toda esta ropa que llevo empapada de sudor y tostarme al sol.

Aquella incitación enardeció a los hombres todavía más. Ya no sentían el calor ni el cansancio, sino la lujuria que se les enroscaba a los hombros brutalmente. Manolo Pelayo quiso desviar el diálogo:

–Ahora llegamos enseguida a un camino de cabila, con higueras. Allí podremos descansar.

–Déme usted agua –pidió Carmen.

–No me queda. López, trae tu cantimplora –López entregó a Carmen la cantimplora. Para beber, ella detuvo el mulo, y los dos se quedaron un poco rezagados.

–Está buena.

–Yo le echo anís, ¿sabe usted? Y está más fresca.

–¿Qué es lo que te gusta a ti más, López? Quiero hacerte un regalo.

–¡Huy! ¿A mí? Pues a mí me gustan... ¡No se lo dirá usted al teniente!

–Claro que no.

–Pues a mí me gustan... las mozas. A mí me gustan las mozas una barbaridad.

–¿Y si se entera Adela?

Otra vez Carmen se incorporó al convoy, que momentos después ganó la cumbre del monte. Dos higueras enclenques –heroicas hilanderas del sol del

"And the others, do they have girlfriends?"

"That one and this one," he said pointing to two of the soldiers, "yes they have. Hey, López, what's your girl's name?"

"Adela."

"That's a pretty name," said Carmen. "She must be pretty."

"Yes…But you're more so."

And López followed the compliment with a metallic, almost obscene guffaw.

"You're very gallant López," she replied. "Don't let Adela find out."

"'Well I er… You see… I…'"

But something outrageous must have occurred to López, because he suddenly became very serious, staring at Carmen's lips, like a fly in a jar of honey.

The heat was suffocating. The track was now a calloused slope, treeless, without grass or even a bird. The mules wearily zigzagged their way up.

"Corporal," exclaimed Carmela, "you know what I'd like to do right now?"

"No, I don't."

"Take off all these sweaty clothes and bathe in the sun."[49]

The men were inflamed even further by her provocative manner. They no longer felt the heat or fatigue, only the carnal desire which brutally coiled itself around their shoulders. Manolo Pelayo wanted to change the subject:

"We're about to reach a tribal track with prickly pear trees. We can rest up there."

"Give me some water," begged Carmen.

"I don't have any left. López, bring your canteen."

López gave Carmen the canteen.

In order to drink, she pulled up the mule, and the two of them lagged behind a little.

"It's good."

"I poured in some anisette, you know? And it makes it fresher."

"What do you like best, López? I want to give you a gift."

"Ah! Me? Well I like… You won't tell the lieutenant!"

"Of course not."

"Well I like… girls. I like girls something terrible."

"And if Adela finds out?"

Once again, Carmen caught up with the convoy, which reached the top of the hill moments later. Two puny prickly pear trees – heroic spinners of

desierto– fabricaban allí un poco de sombra. En la cumbre era la atmósfera más fina, pero se notaba el mismo calor. Sin embargo, la presencia de la cabila, allá abajo, destruía la sensación de soledad que hasta entonces petrificara el paisaje. El cabo dio la voz de ¡alto! y los soldados se tumbaron, rendidos y febriles, después de desabrocharse los correajes.

—Dejad la sombra para la señora —ordenó Pelayo.

—No, no; cabemos todos. No se muevan.

Ella descendió de un salto y fue a sentarse con los soldados, como una llama entre carbones. Después, pidió el estuche de viaje. Con una toalla se secó bien el rostro y se friccionó con colonia la cabeza y los brazos. Pelayo, de pie, inquieto y hosco, la miraba de reojo. Carmen sacó un espejo de plata y un peine, y se peinó.

—A ver: ¿quién quiere colonia? Voy a perfumaros a todos —dijo Carmen—. Primero a ti, López. Ven aquí.

López se acurrucó a sus pies, como un simio. Y Carmen le vació medio frasco en la cabezota salvaje.

—¡Huy! ¡Huy! ¡Cómo pica!

Los perfumó a todos, uno a uno.

—¿Usted no quiere, cabo?

—No.

—Me desprecia. Bueno…

Después se acostó, boca arriba, con las manos a modo de almohada. Toda ella era un vaho sensual. Su pecho, pequeño, palpitaba con fuerza. Los soldados, con el aliento entrecortado, se apretaban a ella, que parecía no darse cuenta del silencioso cerco. López tenía la boca pegada a su tobillo. Pelayo, indignado, gritó:

—Vamos a seguir. ¡Hala!

Carmen le detuvo:

—Otro poquito, cabo. ¡Estoy tan sofocada!

—¡No puede ser! ¡No puede ser!

Manolo Pelayo, frenético, instaba al montón de soldados, que no le hacía caso. El grupo iba haciéndose cada vez más compacto alrededor de Carmen.

—¿Lo oís? ¡A formar! Pero ¿no oís?

No oían. Uno se atrevió a poner la mano en un brazo de Carmen, que se echó a reír, diabólica. Y entonces sucedió algo monstruoso. López, de un brinco, se lanzó sobre Carmen y le aferró los labios con los suyos. Y como si aquélla fuera la señal, todos se abalanzaron sobre la mujer al mismo tiempo, feroces, siniestros, desorbitados, disputándosela a mordiscos, a puñetazos.

the desert sun – had woven a little shade there. On the summit of the hill the atmosphere was clearer; but the heat was noticeably the same. However, the presence of a Moorish village, there down below, destroyed the sensation of solitude, which until then, had petrified the landscape. The corporal ordered "halt!" and after unbuckling their webbing the soldiers collapsed, worn out and fevered.

"Leave the shade for the lady!" ordered Pelayo.

"No, no; there's room for all of us. Don't move."

She jumped down and like a flame among coals, went to sit with the soldiers. Then, she asked for her traveling chest. She dried her face thoroughly with a towel and massaged her head and arms with cologne. Pelayo, surly and anxious, stood looking at her out of the corner of his eye. Carmen took out a silver mirror and a comb, and combed her hair.

"Right; who wants some cologne? I'm going to perfume the lot of you," said Carmen. "First you López. Come here."

López spiraled up onto his feet like a monkey. Carmen emptied half a bottle onto his large, wild head.

"Oh! Oh! It really stings!"

She perfumed them all, one by one.

"Don't you want any corporal?"

"No."

"You're turning me down. Alright…"

Then, she lay down on her back, with her hands forming a pillow. She was one complete vapor of sensuality. Her small breasts heaved powerfully. The soldiers with labored breath, squeezed up to her, she seemed not to be aware of the silent siege. López's was pressing his mouth against her ankle. Pelayo was annoyed and shouted:

"Let's go on. Get up!"

Carmen stopped him:

"Just a little while longer corporal. It's so stifling!"

"This can't be happening! This can't be happening!"

The heaped soldiers were not taking any notice of Manolo Pelayo's frenetic orders. The group were gradually closing around Carmen.

"Do you hear me? Form up! Can't you hear me?"

They did not hear him. One of them dared put his hand on one of Carmen's arms, she began to laugh diabolically. And then something monstrous happened. López suddenly leapt onto Carmen and clamped her lips to his own. And, as though that were the signal, they all fell onto the woman at the same time, ferocious, sinister, confused, hitting, biting and fighting over her.

–¿Qué es eso? ¡López! ¡Martínez!

Manolo Pelayo se echó el fusil a la cara y disparó dos veces. Los alaridos de júbilo se transformaron en gritos de dolor. El grupo se deshizo y todos fueron cayendo uno aquí y otro allá, bañados en sangre. Carmen, hollada, pisoteada, estaba muerta de un balazo en la frente.

"What's this? López! Martínez!"

Manolo Pelayo took up his rifle and fired twice. The howls of pleasure turned into cries of pain. The group broke up and they were falling here and there, bathed in blood. Carmen, trodden on and trampled, lay dead with a bullet through her forehead.

NOTES

1. A blockhouse is a portable, fortified, loopholed construction built to defend an isolated position.
2. The reference to Defoe's *Robinson Crusoe* is obviously an ironic comment about the unkempt appearance of the soldiers who the protagonist and his platoon were replacing. The mention of Robinson Crusoe in the first story of the book should also be read as an intertextual clue to frame Díaz-Fernández's project in *El blocao*. As Helen Tiffin argues, *Robinson Crusoe*, like William Shakespeare's *The Tempest* before it, "was part of the process of 'fixing' relations between Europe and its others" (101, 2005). Defoe offers in this novel a clear allegory of European colonization with its paternalistic appeal for the acculturation of 'savage' peoples. Interestingly, one of the sources of Robinson Crusoe and a widely translated text during the eighteenth century in England is Andalusian scholar and philosopher Ibn Tufayl's twelfth-century narrative *Hayy Ibn Yaqzan*, the story of a man raised in isolation who develops his own understanding of the world out of empirical observation. Unlike Defoe's, Tufayl's text advocates rational thought, empiricism, and hence individual religious independence: the opposite of cultural colonization (Kugler 2012, 35–54). Díaz-Fernández's own text with its aversion to colonialism seems closer to Tufayl's than Defoe's.
3. Spanish conscripts who could afford to pay a quota could opt for shorter, less risky postings while in the army. These were normally the sons of middle and upper class families, and were known as 'cuotas' in Spanish.
4. Tetouan is a city some 42 kilometers from Ceuta in the foothills of the Jebel Dersa, selected as the capital and headquarters of the Spanish High Command, and seat of the *Khalifa* representing the Sultan of Morocco.
5. The Sueca is an old commercial neighborhood in Tetouan. Díaz-Fernández's reference to the brothels in this area should not be confused with the actual Jewish quarter or *mellah*. The Sephardic community was the only sizeable religious minority outside Islam in Morocco, and, as in most Muslim countries, was 'protected' by laws like the discriminatory charter for the minorities or *dhimmi* that dictated how Jews should behave in public (Deshen 1989, 18–9). The existence of *mellahs* in Morocco has been documented since 1438 when the *mellah* of Fes was founded. The *mellah* of Tetouan, founded in 1807, was obviously a more recent development. Coincidentally, Tetouan was also the first city chosen by the Alliance Israélite Universelle (AIU) to open its first school in 1860. The schools of the AIU were among the only schools in the

Spanish Protectorate representing French culture and were strongly linked to educational reform (Laskier 1983, 347–8).
6. Fortified Moorish citadel, normally located on high ground.
7. Cante Jondo: one of the many variants of Flamenco, it is believed to be the most heart-felt expression of this traditional Spanish music.
8. The Picasso Files (the report compiled in 1922 as a result of the Disaster of Annual) described the multiple difficulties encountered by the Spanish army to provide its soldiers with supplies. The inhospitable terrain, the lack of proper transportation vehicles, the fact that the different units were often expected to pick up their own supplies rather than have them issued in their positions, and the existence of corrupt officers overseeing the supply corps, resulted in a chaotic situation where soldiers were usually expected to provide for themselves. The officers also felt that the troops were deployed more quickly and with much better effect if they were not provided with supplies, which meant that the soldiers would have to steal or barter with the locals in order to feed themselves.
9. The narrator's disturbing attraction for Aisha, an underage girl, is but the tip of the iceberg of the sexual trafficking that went on in both the Spanish and French zones. The French had systematically used the kidnapping of young daughters of non-cooperating notables in Algeria as a way of reining in the subversive elements. It was also customary practice to arrest young girls on any pretence to replenish the soldiers' brothels. In the case of Morocco, the age of consent was lowered to facilitate trafficking (Limmoncelli 2010, 128–32).
10. Kaiser Wilhelm II's abdication in November 1918, heralded the fall of the monarchy and the end of World War I. Wilhelm II had been infamous for his inability to control his temper which often led him into serious diplomatic fiascos. Wilhelm was the grandson of Queen Victoria of England, and his belligerence has been interpreted as the result of the ongoing feuds between the different members of the European royal families (Röhl 2005, 137–56). Wilhelm's visit to Tangier in 1905 was viewed as an explicit expression of interest in the colonization of Morocco on the part of Germany; consequently, France and Britain were to be denied the opportunity to jointly dictate the partition of Morocco. This led to the Algeciras Conference which secured France's control of Northern Africa. As a result, Germany's relations with France became strained and only served to reinforce the Franco-British entente. However, as a buffer against British influence in the area, the European powers allowed Spain to gain control of the territory that would become the Spanish Protectorate of Morocco. In 1911, the Second Moroccan Crisis took place during which Germany complained about French military expansion in the region, but only succeeded in further cementing the alliance between France and Britain.

11. In July 1921, Spanish colonial troops were defeated by Abd el-Krim, the Riffian leader who fought against the colonization of the Berber peoples. The defeat of the Spanish army triggered a desperate retreat. As the troops tried to fall back on the city of Melilla, some one hundred kilometers away, they were repeatedly attacked by Berber tribesmen. By the time the survivors reached Melilla, the death toll had risen to over 13,000.

12. The humanization of the watch is parallel to the mechanization of Villabona in Díaz-Fernández's version of a futuristic tale. Marinetti, the fascist, Italian writer who articulated the Futurist doctrine in the early years of the twentieth century had announced the advent of a modern age in which humans and machines would become one. As Günter Berghaus explains, by the 1920s the problems of the rapid mechanization that modernity entailed were much more apparent, and most younger Futurists had mixed feelings about Marinetti's utopian machinism (2009, 28–31). Díaz-Fernández's story is informed by this second phase of Futurism in that the mechanization of Villabona is a critique of the machine of war which ignores its human casualties. 'The Pocket Watch' manages in its deceptively simple narrative to denounce the connivance between early Futurism and Fascist Imperialism.

13. El Raisuni was perceived by the Europeans as a lawless bandit. In contrast with Abd el-Krim, whose rebellion against the Spaniards quickly acquired political significance, El Raisuni's actions, including his short career as the Pasha of Tangier and the kidnaping of American entrepreneur Ion Perdicaris, seem to have been motivated by personal gain. Interestingly, it was precisely the attempt on the part of Commandant-General Manuel Fernández Silvestre to outdo his superior, the High Commissioner of Spanish Morocco Dámaso Berenguer, that led to the Disaster of Annual. Berenguer attacked El Raisuni in 1920, while in 1921, Silvestre ventured out of the secure region surrounding Melilla towards Alhucemas. Abd el-Krim massacred the troops led by Silvestre at Annual (Nerín 2005, 13–14).

Like most Arabic names, the transliteration of his name was highly unstable. Mulai Ahmed Er Raisuni seems to be the correct transliteration of his name, although the following variants are also frequently used: Raisuli, Raissoulli, Rais Uli and Raysuni. There seems to be neither rhyme nor reason as to why some writers prefer to use one variant rather than another. Rosita Forbes, an extremely popular travel writer and adventurer of the time, favors the Spanish variant in her book *El Raisuni. The Sultan of the Mountains*, Ion Perdicaris uses Raisuli in his 1906 article on Morocco for National Geographic, and most French literature refers to him as Raissouli.

14. Díaz-Fernández is referring here to the 'reconquest' of Spanish Morocco by the Spanish army after the Disaster of Annual. Nador was the first major victory, and the occupation of the Magán peninsula was greatly celebrated.

In the context of the national trauma that followed the Disaster of Annual, the narrator's dismissal of the performance of the Spanish army during this campaign must have been extremely shocking to most Spanish and European readers who perceived Abd el-Krim's actions as acts of savage cruelty. Throughout the different campaigns in Morocco, the lack of discipline among the Spanish troops became notorious. Historian Sebastian Balfour explains that both in 1908 and 1909 the disciplinary brigade that took part in the attacks suffered numerous desertions, lacked discipline in the use of ammunition, and caused multiple problems in the rear-guard (2002, 22). While the Spanish army improved its procedures with time, these problems continued to affect the Spanish Protectorate even after the pacification of the territory in 1927. The Spanish army of the time had a disproportionate number of officers which aggravated its lack of efficacy. In fact, one of the issues that led to the rebellion of the Spanish colonial officers, which eventually became the Spanish Civil War, was Spanish Minister of War Manuel Azaña's attempt to reduce the size of the army while trying to secure the loyalty of the remaining officers to the Second Spanish Republic. The 'Ley Azaña', as it came to be known, resulted in the increasing animosity of the *Africanista* officers towards the government (Cardona 1983, 138–44).

15. Seneca, of course, was the victim of Nero's authoritarian rule. Seneca was forced to drink poison after he was wrongly accused of having participated in a conspiracy to overthrow Nero.

16. The R.38 752 rifle or Remington was already an outmoded weapon when *El blocao* was published. Spain, like many European armies adopted the Mauser model 1893, a more modern rifle at the turn of the century, and would continue to use the Mauser for forty-five years (Álvarez 2001, 8–9). The main dailies of the time, however, doubted the ability of the Spanish army to modernize itself as the many entries in the magazine *Blanco y Negro* throughout 1893 indicate (*Blanco y Negro* 23 September, October 21 1893).

17. Díaz-Fernández's visual description here is interesting in its ability to evoke the Orientalist paintings of artists like Mariano Fortuny who initially set out to produce Orientalist depictions of Colonial Morocco, but ended up creating a series of works that were highly critical of the colonial enterprise. A prime example of this is Fortuny's *Battle of Tetouan* in which the traditional Orientalist image of rational, well organized, European troops conquering savage, chaotic, Maghrebian peoples is subverted to suggest that it is precisely the Spanish, colonial army that is instigating chaos (Martín-Márquez 2008, 118–19). The tension between a pro-colonialist, Orientalist art and a realistic, and hence critical, depiction of these Orientalist motives can be traced back to the work of Jenaro Pérez Villaalmil, and was a constant throughout Spanish Orientalist art (Arias-Anglés 2007). Díaz-Fernández seems to be referring to this split within

Spanish Orientalist art when he describes the sun's dismissal of the Moorish part of Tetouan by problematizing the Orientalist representation of Tetouan while emphasizing the ethnocentric bias of the narrator.

18. Alcazaba de los Adives de Tetuán. *Regulares'* barracks were adjacent to it.

19. The narrator's complaints about his 'lack of spirit' or lack of aesthetic sensibility for what seem to be traditional artistic motives, contrast with his newfound sensitivity or rather what we could call aesthetic empathy for more humane subjects. Díaz-Fernández was one of the leading intellectuals who advocated an end to what Spanish philosopher José Ortega y Gasset, referring to avant-garde art, called dehumanized art. Díaz-Fernández wanted to re-humanize art, to bring politics and social concerns back into art. Ortega y Gasset had argued that Romanticism had only produced populist art, Díaz-Fernández wrote an artistic manifesto called 'The New Romanticism' in which he advocated a type of art that did not shy away from populism as long as it could achieve its political goals.

20. Coinage named for Sultan Mulay Hassan, according to Alberto España in his 1954 account of the Spanish Protectorate *La Pequeña Historia de Tánger.*

21. This is a pun on the lack of sexual vigor of the Moor. A 'gatillazo', or the act of shooting a weapon that is not loaded, is slang for a man who is unable to perform sexually.

22. One of the Spanish Protectorate's five administrative regions, covering the Ceuta and Larache area.

23. Series of hills close to Tetouan. From the old Spanish military observation post on Jebel Gorgues' 1126m peak, Ceuta and the Spanish coast are clearly visible. Frederic Jameson has argued that the split consciousness that characterizes Modernist prose comes from the inability to reconcile the many different worlds brought together by European, imperialist expansion (Jameson 1990). In the case of Spain, where the landscape of Spanish Morocco was a continuation of that of the peninsula, Jameson's theory does not seem to obtain.

24. Tribal elder.

25. Name applied to raiding parties whether friendly or hostile to Spain. The term refers also to the large armed convoys organized by the Sultan to travel throughout his kingdom as described by Walter Harris in *Morocco that Was*, but is also used to refer to other armed groups which responded to tribal authorities instead of the king.

26. *Fuerzas Regulares Indígenas* were established in 1911 by the then Lieutenant Colonel Berenguer, modeled after French units of this type in Algeria. These troops provided Spain with tough and determined soldiers for the positions of greatest danger. They were always in the front line and within the first thirty months thirty-five out of the forty-six strong officer corps were casualties. The *Regulares* soldiers of that period were motivated by the pay scales (at that time, 65 pesetas per month), the leadership of their officers and the possibility of

raids and the subsequent booty. A mistake by an officer in command, an ill-timed withdrawal or even the lack of leadership or toughness of an officer, could occasion his death and the soldiers' desertion.

27. Like many women's names in Spanish, 'Angustias' comes from one of Virgin Mary's advocations. In this case, the *Virgen de las Angustias* or Our Lady of Sorrows in reference to Mary's distress at the death of her son.

28. Georges Sorel (1847–1922) author of *Reflexions sur la violence* (Paris: Riviere 1912). He argued that myth and violence played an important role in facilitating syndicalist revolution.

29. In 1924, Largo Caballero, General Secretary of the UGT (the socialist trade union) agreed to collaborate with dictator Primo de Rivera and continued to do so until the end of the dictatorship in 1930. Many in the socialist party considered that the Spanish monarchy should be overthrown by a bourgeois revolution, and that only after this had taken place could a true proletarian state come to power. Collaboration with the dictator would help preserve workers' rights that had been threatened before by the democratic government of the Restoration. The Metalworkers' Union had led violent confrontations with the dictatorship in 1928, year of the publication of *El blocao*. Angustias' criticisms of the narrator's bourgeois origins are representative of the kind of criticism that the Spanish Socialist Party received from its grass roots (*Coming of the Spanish Civil War*. Preston 1994, 22–6).

30. Portable, barrel- shaped receptacle containing waffles, red-colored with 'roulette' top, customers would bet on 'roulette wheel' in order to 'win' one or other type of wafer.

31. Jacinto Guerrero Torres (1895–1951) was an extremely popular composer. His work chronicles the transition from the traditional Spanish zarzuela (a populist form of opera that combines song and dialogue in equal amounts) to the more modern vaudeville. In 1928, Guerrero Torres premiered his vaudeville *Orgia Dorada* a loosely connected sequence of scenes. *Orgia Dorada* included the song 'Soldadito Español' that praises the bravery of the Spanish troops. Guerrero Torres was obviously riding the wave of the Spanish victory over Abd el-Krim in July 1927. After the premiere of *Orgia Dorada*, he was congratulated by Alfonso XIII (Miranda Calvo 1996, 96). Guerrero Torres also contributed in the production of Orientalist representations of the Maghreb as in his instrumentalist piece *Jhaia (Danza Mora)*. Díaz-Fernández's reference to a piano that can only play to the populist, patriotic tune of Guerrero's music is direct criticism of the Spanish people at large who celebrated a war which was against their own interests.

32. Díaz-Fernández was highly critical of the feminist movement that, like the socialist movement to which he belonged, was avidly looking to establish a well-consolidated platform from which to affect social change. In *El Nuevo Romanticismo*, his manifesto for a re-humanized avant-garde, he argues that

feminists were mistaken in their desire to attain bourgeois, democratic rights for women. Political rights amount to little when not accompanied by economic rights. His complaint is that the feminist movement was reifying the same conditions that revolutionaries like him were trying to change. The tone of the critique, with its insistence on an overpowering maternal instinct that clouds Angustias' otherwise fine mind, denotes Díaz-Fernández's own chauvinistic bias. The debate over whether feminism should be independent from the workers' movement occupied many of the discussions among Spanish feminist leaders. Federica Montseny, Minister of Health during the Spanish Second Republic and an anarchist leader, argued that feminism should be integrated in a more comprehensive revolutionary agenda. Lucía Sánchez Saornil, also an anarchist as well as a poet, argued that feminism should remain independent from the workers' struggle (Gómez 2005, 268).

33. The 'Star' pistol was known as the 'sindicalista' or 'trade-unionist' in Spanish because it was the weapon of choice used by trade union activists (Hernández 1980, 194). The 'Star' pistol could be held by a cord, tied to the belt and let down towards the bottom of the leg through a hole in the pants' pocket thereby, making it more difficult to detect if searched.

34. This may be a reference to the 1911 or 1917 general strikes, or any of the multiple attempts to organize a general strike that took place during the 1920s. Both the 1911 and the 1917 general strikes failed due to energetic repression by the government or lack of support from the workers. Socialists were in principle opposed to the general strike in direct confrontation with anarcho-syndicalists who considered the general strike one of their most effective weapons. Julián Besteiro, secretary general of the Spanish Socialist Party between 1925 and 1931, was in principle opposed to the general strike but supported it to protest against the Moroccan War (Meaker 1974, 39). General strikes had been organized since the end of the nineteenth century throughout Europe, although it was the 1905 Great October Strike in Russia that was often referred to as the prime example of a successful revolutionary action. World War I, paradoxically, was one of the main events that contributed to the formation of an international workers movement. Young European men became aware that the war like the miserable conditions in which they worked were promoted by the economic interest of the bourgeoisie. Europe saw an abundance of general strikes between 1917 and 1920 as a result of that (Wrigley 2002, 2–5). Spain did not participate in World War I, but the socialist movement and particularly the anarcho-syndicalist movements were extremely active in the country at the turn of the century. In the case of the 1917 general strike, the momentum for the strike seems to have come from the top rather than from the workers themselves. There seems to be no correlation between the general price rise in the different areas of Spain and the level of participation of each region in the general strike; most significantly, the most acute price rise took place after the

strike (Meaker 1974, 38). This disconnect between political theory, political praxis, and reality on the ground is a familiar theme in Díaz-Fernández's work.

35. Spanish infantry march.

36. *Banderita, Banderita* was one of the songs in Jacinto Guerrero Torres' 1919 musical comedy *Las Corsarias* in which a group of female pirates kidnap men to marry them. The comedy plays on the anxiety about the scarcity of men caused by the Melilla war. After the Barranco del Lobo massacre in 1909, the Spanish Minister of War, Luis Marichalar, had to admit publicly that over 1,000 soldiers had already died in the war (Payne 1967, 110). The high number of casualties and the conscription of working class soldiers – upper class young men were able to pay for safer postings – triggered a week-long revolt in Barcelona known as the *Setmana Tràgica*. The anxiety over the decimation of an entire generation of young men in Spain was also informed by the high number of casualties throughout Europe during World War I.

37. Xauen also Chefchaouen, founded by Moors expelled from Granada under Muley Rachid in 1471. It is some 60 kilometers from Tetouan. Spanish forces under General Berenguer occupied Chefchaouen on October 14 1920.

38. Although Karl Marx did not openly criticize colonialism, socialist and communist parties throughout Europe soon came to the conclusion that capitalism and colonialism worked hand in hand. No clear position against, however, was reached by either of them until well into the twentieth century. In 1925, *Clarté* published a manifesto, 'Appel aux travailleurs intellectuels,' in which many intellectuals associated with the French Communist Party, one being André Breton, called for the end of the Rif War. This was one of several actions organized by the French Communist Party to put an end to the war, although the success of this campaign was very limited. In 1927, a group of prominent political activists founded the League Against Imperialism (LAI) in Brussels as an attempt to create a forum where 'bourgeois' nationalist movements from the colonies and Communists could work together following the Comintern's policy at that time. The LAI imploded soon after it was created due to the Communists' aggressive treatment of dissenters within the group (Derrick 2008, 151–5, 179). Historian Andrée Bachoud argues that, despite the lack of agreement among anti-colonialists and political groups on the left throughout Europe, the Spanish Socialist Party was naturally inclined to take an anti-colonialist position although it never articulated a clear theoretical position that could persuade its European counterparts (Bachoud 1988, 208).

39. Most Moroccan Jews are of Sephardic origin. Many of them belonged to the Jewish communities that left Spain in 1492 after the Spanish Catholic Kings, Ferdinand and Isabella expelled them from their recently unified kingdom. Sephardic Jews speak Haketia, the regional version of Ladino in the Maghreb. Haketia is a transliteration of Hebrew into the Latin alphabet which borrows heavily from Spanish and Arabic. To the Spanish ear, Haketia sounds like the

ancient Spanish spoken in the sixteenth century. When the Spanish soldiers entered Chefchaouen they were welcomed by the Sephardim who greeted them in Haketia (Jensen 2005, 40). One can only imagine the surprise of the Spanish soldiers, many of them illiterate, when, on entering a Moroccan city, they met with a group of European-looking men and women who spoke to them in what sounded like medieval Spanish.

40. Osinaga, Captain of Engineers. Lieutenant Andrés Fernández Osinaga was initially based in Gijón, Spain; he first served with I Mixed Infantry Regiment in Ceuta in 1910 (DO January 19, 1910). In 1912 he arrived in the Protectorate with the new Spanish Consul, and was tasked to prepare a blueprint for building development in the Tetouan area. (*La Vanguardia* July 4, 1912) He took part in the excavation of Tetouan's *mazmorras* – subterranean cells at Bab Scuda/ Calle San Fernándo, which had formerly held Europeans captured by Barbary pirates. Author of *Locomotores de Vapor Recalentado*. He is buried in a plain grave in the military cemetery in Tetouan, Morocco.

41. General Felipe Alfau was the first High Commissioner of Spanish Morocco. He considered himself to be an enlightened career soldier, by which he meant a highly educated soldier. He attempted to control the area by engaging the tribes in negotiations which they interpreted as a sign of weakness. In the end Alfau adopted some of the harsher methods, like the decapitation of prisoners, who had provided valuable service to the tribal leaders and the colonialists alike. In a telegram to General Luque, Spanish Minister of War, Alfau argued that decapitation was highly recommended because of the psychological impact it had on the Moroccan population, but that the Spanish army should not publicly admit to having decapitated its enemies. General Luque responded saying that he would take care of lying about it if necessary (Balfour 2002, 94).

42. The cultivation of cannabis in Morocco probably dates back to the Arab invasions of the fourteenth century although no historical record exists. Interestingly, the cultivation and consumption of cannabis remained unregulated until Sultan Hassan I legalized its cultivation in the Ketama region in 1890. Europeans of all economic and educational backgrounds had been fascinated by cannabis since Napoleon's soldiers brought it back with them from Egypt (Booth 2004, 65–162). In 1830, several French Romantic writers like Baudelaire, Gautier, and Moreau founded the *Club des Hashischins* where they experimented with the use of the drug. Cannabis consumption was also popular with Spanish writers and intellectuals at the turn of the twentieth century. In 1919, Ramón María del Valle-Inclán wrote *La pipa de Kif,* a collection of poems inspired by his experiences with cannabis. For Valle-Inclán and many of the writers of his generation that became interested in cannabis, the mind-altering effects of the drug were associated with their revolutionary political persuasion. The idea was that accessing new perceptions of reality would enable them to imagine a new world in which a revolution could eventually take place (Fuentes 1987,

178–9). Cannabis was also popular with the Spanish conscripts in Morocco.

43. A great part of the commercial exchanges that took place in the Spanish Protectorate were on the black market. This type of under-the-table business not only affected the officers who inflated the price of supplies, but regular merchants and businessmen. The extent of the corruption has been studied by historian Rosa María Madariaga in her book *Marruecos, ese gran desconocido: breve historia del Protectorado Español* (2013). There was also a black market in the French zone, and French officers "augmented their 'Caisse Noire' by discreet trade on the black market during the period of rationing" or secured the loyalty of the kaids by supplying them with goods that they could trade on the black market (Bidwell 1973, 89, 186).
44. These words about the militia appear in *El alcalde de Zalamea*, although the literal quote comes from *Para vencer a amor* III, 169 c (I, XIV) a play also written by Spanish poet and playwright Calderón de la Barca. The Spanish poet praises the heroic militias associated with the expansion of the Spanish empire from the fifteenth to seventeenth centuries. By having the captain quote Calderón's poem well after the Spanish empire had vanished, Díaz-Fernández is subtly criticizing the delirium of grandeur that characterized the post-imperial, expansion of Spain in Morocco. The Spanish Protectorate in Morocco was not exactly a result of Spanish military power, but a concession on the part of the European powers to maintain the international status quo in the area. Great Britain did not want to see France diminish its control over the Strait of Gibraltar and favored a weak European power, Spain, in neighboring Morocco. Allowing Spain to take hold of Northern Morocco had the additional advantage of keeping Germany out of the region. Spanish Dictator Miguel Primo de Rivera had long hoped to be able to exchange Ceuta for Gibraltar, so the idea of a Spanish Protectorate was of interest even to those in Spain who were not, at least initially, seduced by the prospect of colonial expansion in Morocco (Balfour 2002, 94).
45. The advent of the industrial revolution altered the way in which individuals interacted with each other within family units, their communities and with their environment. The birth and development of the ecologist movement was closely related to the reaction of workers and intellectuals against the unsanitary conditions in which the former had to live in the cities. The anarchist movement throughout Europe became interested in alternative lifestyles that facilitated a return to a natural balance. In Spain, where anarchism became especially popular, there were numerous institutions like the Catalan *Amics del Sol* that published magazines like *Acción Naturista* or *Eugenia* devoted to naturist and hygienist practices. This early environmentalism was concerned with animal rights in as much as the degradation of nature affected the working classes (Masjuan-Bracons 2000, 435–40). Artists like Miguel de Unamuno and Buñuel were interested in the naturist movement throughout their lives.

Unamuno wrote a poem titled 'Elegía en la muerte de un perro' in which the concern for animal feelings is clearly expressed. Buñuel's sensitivity towards animal rights, however, did not develop in the same way.

Díaz-Fernández's story describes how colonialist ideology overlaps with animal cruelty. The story is particularly effective in its suggestion that animal cruelty is only steps removed from cruelty to colonial subjects. Interestingly, it is Ojeda, the country boy in the platoon, who dares to confront Lieutenant Compañón. Ojeda's empathy for the dog is understandable because of his rural background which leads us to assume that he is used to dealing with animals. In the context of the environmentalist movement that was promoted by anarchist groups, Ojeda also represents a pre-modern man, an individual that has not been corrupted by industrialization. Ojeda's outrage at the lieutenant Compañón's cruelty shows that his moral compass has not been distorted by modernity.

46. The Yebala region was being secured in 1921 by General Dámaso Berenguer while General Silvestre tried to reach Alhucemas Bay. Silvestre was eventually surrounded and defeated by Abd el-Krim in what came to be known as the Disaster of Annual.

47. As he does throughout *El blocao*, but more explicitly in this story, Díaz-Fernández is subverting the reader's expectations. Sensationalistic chronicles of the attacks of Moroccan rebels on Spanish colonial troops became a sub-genre during the 1920s and 30s. Serialized as well as in paperback, affordable editions of stories included Juan Ferragut's *La misma sangre* (1921) and *Memorias de un legionario* (1921), Carlos Micó's *Lupo Sargento* (1922) and *El camillero de la legión* (1922), and Antonio Hoyos' *Bajo el sol enemigo* (1922). These works sought to capture the nascent mass market by providing lurid details of the events in Morocco.

48. It is important to notice that Díaz-Fernández is subverting turn of century imagery that represented Arabs as savagely lascivious. The image of the Moor as a sexual predator was well established in the European/Spanish imaginary. Throughout Europe, captivity narratives told stories of men and women being abducted and raped by Moors. As Juan Goytisolo explains in his *Crónicas sarracinas* the image of the Moor in Spanish literature has always expressed the fear of an invader who is both cruel and lascivious, the Moorish invasion has often been described as the rape of the Iberian Peninsula.

49. Sunbathing was supposedly popularized by Coco Chanel, although this new fashion was probably a side-effect of the nascent upper-class sea-side tourism that developed at the end of the nineteenth century. Carmen's desire to sunbathe defines her as a modern woman at a time when Paris was still the center of all things fashionable (Chaney 2012, 209–10).